Configuring Windows 2008 R2 Web Server

Configuring Windows 2008 R2 Web Server

**A step-by-step guide to building
Internet servers with Windows**

Sergey Nosov

Nosov, Sergey, 1976-.

Configuring Windows 2008 R2 web server / Sergey Nosov.
    236 p. 22 cm.

ISBN-13: 978-1-47921-630-7

1. Microsoft Windows server. 2. Computer network resources. I. Title.

QA76.76.O63
005.4'476–dc22

www.orderfactory.com

The following names are trademarks or registered trademarks in the United States or other countries. Microsoft, Active Directory, Internet Explorer, NetShow, SharePoint, SQL Server, Visual Basic, Visual Studio, Visual Web Developer, Windows, Windows Media, Windows NT, Windows PowerShell, Windows Server, and Windows Vista of Microsoft Corporation. Linux of Linus Torvalds. Apache of The Apache Software Foundation. MySQL of Oracle Corporation. AMD and Opteron of Advanced Micro Devices, Inc. Intel and Xeon of Intel Corporation. Zend and Zend Server of Zend Technologies Ltd. Google of Google Inc. Other product and company names mentioned herein may be the trademarks of their respective owners. We use the names only in editorial fashion and to the benefit of the trademark owners, with no intention of infringement.

This book expresses the author's views and opinions. The information is provided on an "as is" basis without any express, statutory, or implied warranties. Neither the author nor the publisher will be held liable for any loss or damages caused or alleged to be caused either directly or indirectly by this book.

"Configuring Windows 2008 R2 Web Server" is an independently published book and is not affiliated with, nor has it been authorized, sponsored, or otherwise approved by Microsoft Corporation. Windows is a registered trademark of Microsoft Corporation in the United States and other countries.

Cover design by: Matthias Nolte

Contents

vi

Preface

In this book we are concerned with building and configuring a single stand-alone web server. This web server will be used to serve email, host web sites and web services that take advantage of various modern technologies, and to run infrastructure associated with Internet presence.

In particular, information presented here will be of interest to companies and individuals renting 1U or 2U datacenter spaces, or running Internet or intranet servers in-house. If you are managing a whole rack of equipment, setting up a web-farm, or have your own datacenter, your requirements will be somewhat different; yet, we are sure, you will still find some of the individual chapters useful.

Traditionally web servers run on various flavors of UNIX, including Sun Solaris and Linux. Starting with Windows 2000, Microsoft Windows has been recognized as a viable platform for Internet facing servers, and in this book the operating system of choice is Windows Web Server 2008 R2.

Before you begin

Selecting Hardware

So, you have decided (or have been given a task) to configure a web server using Windows 2008 R2. Sometimes you have to work with what you have got, but if you have a say in what kind of hardware is to be used, then a little bit of planning ahead can be very beneficial.

Web servers are expected to run for years with little or no downtime. This dictates a few aspects that make server hardware different from that of desktop computers. Ample cooling is important; if a fan seizes to work, the server should be able to sense that, notify you, and still have cooling capacity to continue working while waiting for the failed component to be replaced.

Processor and Chipset

You may begin by selecting the processor (CPU or central processing unit), or multiple processors, for your server. The exact performance specifications will depend on your particular needs. Keep in mind that video performance, for example, is usually not important for a server – unless special software you plan to run is capable of utilizing a graphics processing unit (GPU) to perform calculations – high input-output throughput, on the other hand, is important. You can search the Internet and read current reviews to help selecting your hardware platform.

Processor manufactures have separate lines of server processors to help distinguishing them from processors meant for desktop and other use. Such, the chip manufacturer Intel has the line of *Intel Xeon* processors, its competitor Advanced Micro Devices (AMD) similarly has the line of *AMD Opteron* processors.

Please do not forget that Windows 2008 R2 requires 64-bit architecture. The last version of Windows Server that could run on 32-bit computers was 2008 (the release before R2). As such you will need a processor that supports ether AMD *x86-64* (also known as *AMD64*) or Intel *EMT64T* (also known as *Intel 64*) instruction set.

There is a special version of Windows 2008 R2 for Intel *Itanium* architecture (also known as *IA-64*). You must have specific reasons to select this platform, especially since Microsoft has announced that Windows Server 2008 R2 would be the last version of Windows Server to support the Intel Itanium processor and associated original equipment manufacturer (OEM) server platforms.

Once you selected the processor, you will find out that there is one or more chipsets compatible with this processor. Chipsets consist of one or several microchips that facilitate microprocessor's communication with other parts of the system. These microchips come soldered to the motherboard, while processors are almost always removable.

While in more recent designs there is only one chipset, also known as *platform controller hub* (PCH); older designs made a distinction between the so called "Northbridge" and "Southbridge" chipsets that function in tandem.

ECC Registered Memory

ECC Registered memory modules are recommended for servers. These differ from desktop memory by adding redundant memory storage for error-checking and some error-correcting, and by including a register for more stable operation and scalability. To be functional, ECC memory must be supported by the processor. Most server grade processors support ECC, while many processors meant for desktop computers, do not.

Memory Type, Speed, and Voltage

A great variety of memory modules exist. Some, such as Dual inline package (DIP) chips form the first PC computers and single in-line memory modules (SIMs) from the 80's and 90's have been depreciated. A few short-lived memory packaging types have appeared through the years, such as single in-line pin package (SIP), Rambus in-line memory module (RIMM), and others.

The prevalent memory package of today is dual in-line memory module or DIMM. There are more than a dozen of different types of DIMMs which are distinguished by the number of pins and further by name and layout. For example, 240-pin DIMMs are available in three flavors: DDR2 SDRAM, DDR3 SDRAM, and FB-DIMM DRAM.

These three flavors of 240-pin DIMMs are incompatible with each other, and they are made physically slightly different so that the wrong type cannot be installed.

DDR stands for *double data rate*, SDRAM stands for *synchronous dynamic random access memory*, and FB-DIMM DRAM stands for *fully buffered DIMM dynamic random-access memory*.

Let us take the DDR3 SDRAM and drill down further to examine what is available.

Memory can be characterized by the maximum data rate of the individual memory chips expressed in mega transfers per second (MT/s), or by peak transfer rate of the whole memory module expressed in megabytes per second (MB/s). As such, we can see one retailer referring to a memory module as DDR3-1333 while another retailer calling the same memory module PC3-10600. Where 1333 is the data rate in MT/s, and 10600 is approximately the transfer rate in MB/s.

Higher sped memory modules are more than happy to work at slower speeds. For example, if your motherboard calls for PC3-8500 memory modules with DDR3-1066 chips you can install the higher rated PC3-10600 memory modules with DDR3-1333 chips, and you will experience no problems whatsoever.

What can pose a problem is voltage required to drive particular memory modules.

DDR3 SDRAM, for instance, comes in three voltage varieties:

- 1.5 V DDR3 for PC3 modules
- 1.35 V DDR3L for PC3L modules
- 1.25 V DDR3U for PC3U modules

Your server motherboard and processor combination may support memory modules of specific voltage, then you have no choice but to purchase memory modules of that voltage, or it may support a variety of different memory voltages. In the latter case you need to pick one voltage and stick to it, as mixing memory modules of different voltages is prohibited or discouraged in most cases. Other things being equal, lower voltage memory modules will run cooler and consume less electricity.

Memory Timings

Examining the specs of a memory module in more details we come to memory timings. These are often missing from retailer product descriptions, but you can go to the memory manufacturer's web site and search by exact memory module model number to get this information.

For random access memory, with data storage organized in rows and columns, timings are normally expressed in three numbers, such as 7-7-7, or in one number (which is the first of the previous three) written as CL7 or similar.

Right away let us say that the lower the numbers the better. These numbers represent delays in clock cycles the computer has to wait during different stages of accessing the memory. The following table contains brief descriptions of these three numbers in order.

Symbol	Description	Example
CL or *tCAS*	CAS Latency	7
tRCD	RAS to CAS Delay	7
tRP	RAS Pre-charge	7

As you can see from the descriptions, the main timing settings are related to Row Access Strobe (RAS) and Column Address Strobe (CAS) signaling.

There are other timing parameters in addition to the three we just discussed; some of the more referenced ones you can see in the following table

Symbol	Description	Example
tRAS	Cycle Time	20
CR	Command Rate	1
tRFC	Row Refresh Cycle Time	59

Memory Ranks and Channels

While purchasing memory modules for your server, besides the obvious requirement to get the correct type of modules, you need to keep in mind two less obvious memory configuration characteristics: rank and channels.

Rank is the number of distinct data areas on a memory module. DIMM memory is commonly manufactured in Single Rank (SR), Dual Rank (DR), and Quad Rank (QR) configurations, with one, two, and four such distinct data areas on each module.

Imagine having a Single Rank memory module. Now take the same number of memory chips that is already on the module and solder the new chips to the same data and address lines. We just created a Dual Rank memory module; alas, we cannot access both of these memory data areas simultaneously; only one rank on a memory module is active at a time. A special chip select (CS) signal is used to indicate which rank to activate.

With some types of memory, the rank is less important. With other types of memory, the total number of ranks is limited, and once that number is reached, no more memory can be added to the server even when it still has empty memory slots available. Oftentimes, when using higher rank memory modules or mixing modules of different ranks, the server has to downgrade memory access speeds.

Read the server or the motherboard manual to see configurations compatible with your setup.

Memory Channels is a concept complete opposite to Memory Ranks. Where by adding ranks to a memory module we divide the memory to chunks that cannot be accessed simultaneously; with memory channels we double, triple, quadruple, and so on memory access lines, so that two, three, or more memory modules can be accessed simultaneously in a single memory bank.

If you server supports multi-channel architecture, basically it means that for optimal performance you need to install memory in sets of identical modules. For dual-channel architecture – in sets of two, for triple-channel architecture – in sets of three, and so on.

A special note on servers with multiple physical processors: check if all the processors connect to the same pool of memory (as in Symmetric Multiprocessing Systems) or if each of the installed processors requires at least one of its proprietary memory banks to be populated (as in systems built under the Non-Uniform Memory Access methodology).

Remote Server Management

Intelligent Platform Management Interface (IPMI) allows monitoring independent from operating system. Some servers support keyboard, video, and mouse (KVM)-over-LAN and virtual media over LAN which can be used for complete firmware and software configuration, including Basic Input Output System (BIOS) options and operating system installation. It is best to use IPMI features over a dedicated network channel. Attaching IPMI to an unprotected public network is a security risk. Instead, choose Virtual Private Network (VPN) or some other secure method of connection.

The management capabilities we just described are referred to as *out-of-band management* or *lights-out management* (since the administrator has access regardless of whether the server is powered on). Conversely, *in-band management* is the management methodology that relies on software running under, or as a part of, the operating system.

Windows Server 2008 R2 comes with its own range of in-band management capabilities.

Formerly known as Terminal Services used in Remote Administration Mode this subsystem is now referred to as Remote Desktop Services or RDS.

With RDS you can connect to the server from a remote computer via Remote Desktop Connection. This opens up a window on the remote computer, that can be expanded to fit full screen, and in that window is your server's desktop that you can manipulate with keyboard and mouse, open applications, and use command line tools or dialog boxes, just as if you were sitting in front of the physical server.

With RDS you can also attach local clipboard, printers, ports, smart cards, plug and play devices, and drives. Attaching drives allows you to copy and paste files between the server and your local machine right in the Windows Explorer opened in the Remote Desktop Connection window.

In comparison to the KVM-over-LAN IPMI access, RDS require Windows operating system to be up and running. As such, RDS do not give you access to computer screens that appear before Windows is started; those include motherboard and storage controller BIOS configuration screens, boot options, and OS installation and recovery consoles.

The RDS advantages are relative ease of configuration and better multimedia performance.

Server Storage

At the time of this writing, the interface of choice for local server hard drives is the Serial Attached SCSI (SAS). Serial ATA (SATA or Serial Advanced Technology Attachment) interface may be used in more budget oriented servers with less stringent storage requirements.

In comparison to their desktop counterparts, server (enterprise grade) hard drives are likely to have additional sensors and specifically tuned firmware settings. In the manufacturer specifications, you may wish to pay attention to the mean time between failure (MTBF) figures; expressed in hours.

Be especially careful when selecting hard drives that will function in hardware arrays. In order to prevent erroneously marking a disk as failed while the drive's built-in error recovery is in progress, most storage array controllers use the feature called error recovery control (ERC), time-limited error recovery (TLER), or command completion time limit (CCTL). Many desktop hard-drives do not have this feature or have it disabled.

Optical Drives

Here is a story that actually happened. We had a high-quality 2U server collocated in a datacenter for nine years. In those nine years the server performed superbly and only needed one fan and one hard drive replaced.

All of the sudden the server developed unexplained hang-ups. We replaced the server with a new one, and brought the old one in-house.

In order to better understand how servers fail and to improve selection of hardware in the future, we decided to diagnose the server and find the cause of the hang-ups. We could describe the problem as follows.

Randomly, with bias towards periods of reduced load and lower ambient temperatures, the server would become unresponsive anywhere from a few hours to a couple of weeks from being turned on. After the freeze, all the lights (power fail, overheat, IDE channel, power), except network activity, on the front panel would be turned on. The network activity light would continue to flash corresponding to activity on the channel.

There was no video output, the keyboard was frozen (Num Lock – On and would not toggle), the reset switch would not work, nether would the power switch (even holding the power switch for extended period of time did nothing).

The Windows operating system on the server had been configured to create Kernel memory dump on failure. But no memory dump was created in our case. There was also nothing suspicious in the Windows event logs. The only out of ordinary event reported was an event number 6008, unexpected shutdown.

The Desktop Management Interface (DMI) event log in the server BIOS was empty. Monitoring of system temperatures, voltages, and fan speeds did not reveal anything wrong.

Even though the server passed extensive memory tests, we replaced memory modules, but this did not fix the issue. We contacted the server manufacturer and explained what was going on, but the manufacturer could not help us, short of sending the server to them; we decided to tackle the issue ourselves.

We run short and long hard drive tests. We also run Windows *sfc /scannow* and *chkdsk* tests. None of the tests revealed anything wrong. One component at a time, we replaced the motherboard, power supplies, power cords, CPUs, and the hard-drive backplane. When we disconnected the optical drive, the server stopped freezing.

The optical drive itself appeared fully operational. It would work and it would read disks just fine; bit it was the cause of the random server hangs.

Ask yourself if you need an optical drive in your server. Perhaps you plan on mailing optical disks to the datacenter so the datacenter personnel can put those disks in for you. If not, consider not including an optical drive in your server. A portable optical drive can be connected via USB interface when needed. The fewer components you have in the server the fewer points of potential failure there are.

On the day these words were written one of our office desktop computers would not power up. A quick examination of add-on boards revealed that a capacitor blew on the TV tuner board. Without the board the computer powered up and continued normal functioning. Being an office commuter; nobody ever had any use for the TV tuner.

If your server already has an optical dive, you may wish to simply disconnect it. Disconnect both data and power cables, and tuck or zip-tie the cables neatly, out of the way. Unless you have appropriate cover plate to close the bay opening, leave the drive in the server, so that not to alter the air flow.

Server Maintenance and Upgrades

Reliability, long useful life, and capacity for monitoring prevail in the selection of server hardware. Server performance, however, is also important. You will need to estimate how much processor speed is required, how many processor cores would be beneficial for your system, how fast your storage devices need to be, and how much random access memory (RAM) you can take advantage of.

Allowing for hardware upgrades can be a smart move. You could add processors if the motherboard allows for it and the processors are compatible. You could add additional memory modules, when you start seeing a lot of hard faults, meaning the operating system had to swap information between disk and memory, and additional RAM would be beneficial. You could add a high performance disk controller or a zero-channel RAID card, to unload disk operations from the main processors. For many types of disk access, adding additional stripe volumes increases performance. You could also replace disks with faster ones, or even replace magnetic disks with solid state memory.

Do not fall into the trap of planning your server upgrades too far in advance, though. Ten years out, those processors you are paying over $1000 each now, could be $50 a pair on eBay. And in five years more, you could be hard pressed to find components for your system at all.

Consider having spare parts on hand. Once a server is up and running the first components to go are usually those with moving parts. That means hard drives and fans. Plan ahead how fast you can get replacements. Since fans are relatively inexpensive, it is a good idea to have some, of the correct types and sizes, as spares. When fans go out the server internal temperature raises, and that in turn causes other components to overheat and potentially fail. As such, when you receive a notification from the server that a fan failed, get it fixed right away.

Do not also forget about components with internal fans, namely power supplies. A server might have redundant power supplies.

When one of the power supplies fails, the server keeps on working, and you have a chance to swap in a new power supply without stopping the server.

RAID Configuration

While server (enterprise grade) grade hard drives are expected to last longer in server environment, hard drives are always a typical point of failure. The prudent strategy is to be ready for any given hard drive to fail at any given time. Redundant Array of Independent Disks (RAID) is a storage technology very well suited to help with this.

RAID allows for multiple physical hard drives (or other types of storage devices, such as solid-state drives) to be combined into logical units of different RAID levels. Some of these RAID levels exhibit data redundancy characteristics, meaning loss of any single physical hard drive will not lead to the loss of data.

The simplest redundant RAID level is RAID Level 1, also called a mirrored array. A minimum of two hard drives are required to create a RAID Level 1. Information is written, or mirrored, to both of the hard drives. Thus, when one of the hard drives fails, the server can keep on working, using the information from the good drive, until the failed drive is replaced and the mirror is rebuilt.

Redundant arrays are not the only types of arrays RAID is capable of. Another type is striped arrays. Similarly to mirrored arrays, a simplest striped array, or Raid Level 0, contains two physical hard drives. In RAID 0, however, the information is not duplicated; the information is written across the hard drives. This increases performance (as the system can write or read a portion of information to or from one hard drive, while another portion of information is read or written to or from another hard drive), however RAID 0 arrays provide no fault tolerance; the loss of any single hard drive in a RAID 0 array leads to the loss of the entire array.

RAID 0 may contain any number of hard drives starting with two. Note that the higher is the number of hard drives in a RAID 0 array the higher is the likelihood of the data failure, as any one hard drive in the array going down destroys the whole array.

RAID arrays do not have to contain physical hard drives; they can also contain other RAID arrays. Such arrays are known as nested or hybrid arrays. A versatile way to increase input-output (I/O) performance of a server storage subsystem is to combine RAID Level 1 arrays into a RAID Level 0 array (or the other way around, RAID Level 0 arrays into a RAID Level 1 array). These arrays are often referred to as RAID 10 (a stripe of mirrors) or RAID 01 (a mirror of stripes).

There are other types of arrays besides 0 and 1, but RAID 0 and RAID 1 are the only types that can be built with two disks minimum. RAIDs 2 through 5 require three disks minimum, and RAID 6 requires four disks minimum.

Levels 2 and 3 striped arrays call for synchronization of disk spindle rotation, and as such not normally used in web servers built with off-the shelf components.

Raid Levels 4 and 5 contain a minimum of three disks. In RAID 4, one of the disks is dedicated to store parity information, the information that can be used to recreate or rebuild data in case one of the other drives fails. In RAID Level 5 the parity information is distributed among all the drives in the array (thus eliminating the potential bottleneck of RAID 4 of always requiring going to a single hard drive to write parity information).

While slower, RAIDs 4 and 5 are more space efficient than RAID 1; they can still recover from a single hard drive failure. Keep in mind that when a hard drive with non-parity data fails in RAID 4 or 5 (that is any hard drive in RAID 5), the I/O performance further decreases, until a replacement hard drive is installed and the array is rebuilt to the healthy state.

RAID Level 6 distributes the double of parity information of RAID level 5. RAID 6 requires a minimum of four hard drives and it retains data integrity with any two hard drives failing. RAID 6 arrays became more popular as capacities of hard drives grew (and as the time needed to recover grew together with the capacities of hard drives).

Higher RAID levels can also be nested. As such, RAID Levels 50, 51, 05, 53, 60, and 61 are among the few used. Note, that there can be multiple levels of RAID nesting, making, for instance,

RAID Level 100 possible, when striping two RAID 10 arrays, in turn creating a hybrid array of hybrid arrays.

Once you decide what RAID level or levels to implement on your server, you need to decide if you will be using a software RAID or a hardware RAID (or a combination of thereof).

A software RAID is RAID subsystem implemented utilizing the main computer processor and resources and without any additional hardware. Windows 2008 R2 supports software RAID Levels 0, 1, and 5. For example, to create a RAID 1, install the needed number of disks in your system, then go to the Disk Management (Server Manager – Storage – Disk Management), convert your data disk to a dynamic disk (if it is not already), then click on the data volume, select "Add Mirror...", and follow the instructions to create a mirror volume on the unused disk.

Do not configure your system or boot volume on Windows 2008 R2 software RAID Level 5 array. RAID Level 1 can be configured for system and boot volumes. Use identical disks when mirroring system or boot volumes.

A hardware RAID is RAID subsystem that is implemented using additional hardware components. Those components could be an add-on card, or additional hardware built into the server motherboard. The best hardware RAID controllers have their own dedicated processor, cache, capable I/O interface, and implement the required levels of storage array organization as well as other features such as hot swap and hot spare.

Hot swap allows for removal and replacement of hard-drives without turning the server off beforehand. Be extra careful if you do that while replacing a failed hard drive in an array. Removing a wrong hard drive can be disastrous.

Hot spare function allows you to install one or more hard drives that will be on standby. When a hard drive from a redundant array fails, the hot spare hard drive replaces it automatically (given that the hot spare is of sufficient size), and the redundancy of the array is restored without human intervention.

Be aware of so called Fake-RAID controllers. Even though these are hardware RAID controllers, they work by taxing heavily the main server resources, negating the primary benefit of hardware RAID of unloading storage operations to dedicated hardware. Fake-RAID cards can be identified by low prices, unclear specifications, and by having no option of battery backup unit (BBU) or zero maintenance cache protection (ZMCP) – as Fake-RAIDs do not have dedicated cache.

When selecting hardware RAID make sure to study specifications and read performance test results.

Updating Firmware

So you have your brand-spanking-new, or new to you, server sitting in front of you (or somewhere where you can communicate to the server via a full fidelity IMPI connection), and you are about to install the operating system on it. This is the perfect time to load latest and greatest firmware from the manufacturers of various hardware components inside the server.

Have you noticed that firmware updates often carry warnings not to apply them unless you experience problems? How do you know if you experience problems if you have not installed anything yet? I say, just spend a few minutes now, and not worry about it later. This way, if you do experience problems, you will know that it is not because your firmware is outdated.

Typical components with updatable firmware include motherboards, optical drives, storage controllers, and various add-on cards. Sometimes updated firmware is available for hard drives.

While you are downloading firmware updates, it is a good idea to also download latest drivers to have them on-hand when you install the operating system. As drivers and firmware updates are often located in the same area of manufacturer web sites, you can save some time by not searching for your specific hardware twice.

A controversial topic is so called cross-flashing. That is updating a hardware component of one brand using firmware released by another manufacturer.

Let us say, a company XXX creates a chipset that it makes available for other companies to implement in their products. Companies

YYY and ZZZ both implement the chipset from the company XXX and start selling their products. So far so good; only some time down the road company ZZZ keeps up with firmware updates and makes latest firmware available to its customers, while company YYY fails to do the same. What do you do if you purchased a product made by company YYY?

If you decided to cross-flash, you obtain firmware from ZZZ (or even directly from XXX), and attempt flashing it to your YYY hardware. This is risky. As, first of all, there can be confusion between different model numbers. And, second, doing such firmware update can invalidate your warranty.

Be especially careful in cases where paid updates are available to unlock some of the hardware features; at the very least, try to find other people who have performed cross-flashing of the same hardware, and inquire what their results where.

Installing Windows

Now you are ready to start the Operating System installation. During the installation you are asked the usual, language to install, time and currency format, keyboard or input language, and the flavor of operating system to install. We chose Windows Web Server 2008 R2 (Full Installation).

Select the operating system you want to install

Operating system	Architecture	Date modified
Windows Server 2008 R2 Standard (Full Installation)	x64	11/21/2010
Windows Server 2008 R2 Standard (Server Core Installation)	x64	11/21/2010
Windows Server 2008 R2 Enterprise (Full Installation)	x64	11/21/2010
Windows Server 2008 R2 Enterprise (Server Core Installation)	x64	11/21/2010
Windows Server 2008 R2 Datacenter (Full Installation)	x64	11/21/2010
Windows Server 2008 R2 Datacenter (Server Core Installation)	x64	11/21/2010
Windows Web Server 2008 R2 (Full Installation)	x64	11/21/2010
Windows Web Server 2008 R2 (Server Core Installation)	x64	11/21/2010

Description:
This option installs the complete installation of Windows Server. This installation includes the entire user interface, and it supports all of the server roles.

After accepting the license terms, we are given a choice to do an upgrade or a completely new installation. We prefer to do fresh installation to an empty disk. By default, install will maximize the size of your system partition; but if you prefer another arrangement, you can manually create a partition of specified size right through the "Where do you want to install Windows?" dialog box (to do so, click on advanced options, and then on the "New" shortcut).

Install will then copy Windows files, expand them, and perform installation routines. The setup will require restarting your server a couple of times before it is ready for first use. Once that happens the first thing you are asked to do is to change the Administrator

user password. You also have an option to create a password reset floppy disk or USB flash drive.

Please note, that you can create additional administrator users,
but do not delete the built-in administrator account, as built-in
accounts carry special properties that do not pass through to users you create manually.

You can however rename the Administrator account. Open the
Local Users and Groups manager (you can reach it by going to
the Start – Administrative Tools – Server Manager, and then
expanding "Local Users and Groups" under "Configuration" in
the Server Manager tree, or by going to Start – Run..., typing
LUSRMGR.MSC, and clicking the OK button).

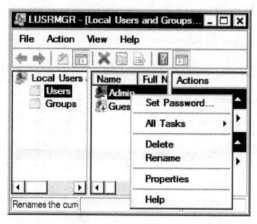

Find the Administrator user under "Users", right click on it, and
select "Rename."

After install, Windows Server 2008 R2 automatically launches
the Initial Configuration Tasks window (you can disable it, by
checking the "Do not show this window at logon" box at the bottom of the window).

The first task listed on the Initial Configuration Tasks window
is "Activate Windows." You are required to activate Windows
within 30 days after installing. You can do it right away, or you
can wait until you have everything installed and configured, so
that you do not have to activate multiple times in case you need
to kill your installation and reload everything from scratch. Also

mind the automatic activation, which by default is triggered in three days after Windows install.

Once you exceed a certain number of activations on your copy of Windows, you will not be able to activate it online and will have to do it by phone, which is less convenient but still perfectly doable.

Another shortcut the Initial Configuration Tasks window offers is to Windows Update, which can also be reached from the Start – All Programs menu. Keeping your server up to day is very important, and Windows Update is a huge help in this regard.

When you use the Windows Update for the first time, the amount of updates can be staggering, and require a lot of individual downloads and restarts. Here is how to speed-up this process a little. First check the version of your Windows service pack, if one is installed then on your "Control Panel\System and Security\System" window (which can be reached by clicking the Start button, then right-clicking on "Computer", and choosing "Properties"), in the Windows edition section, you will see "Service Pack 1" or whatever is the service pack currently installed.

Check Microsoft web site as to the latest service pack available for your version of Windows. If it is higher than what you have installed, you can proceed to download and install the entire service pack. If you are going to the latest service pack anyway, this way you will not be wasting time on various individual pre-service pack updates.

Same logic applies to Internet Explorer. Instead of patching up the version that came with the Windows installation, download the latest version of Internet Explorer, and then configure your automatic Windows Updates.

Keep in mind that Windows Update can keep up to date not only the Operating System but other Microsoft products as well, if you have any on your server; Microsoft SQL server is one of such products. Do not forget to turn the option to give updates for Microsoft products in Windows Update settings.

Windows Server Backup

One of the first things I like to do after installing an operating system is to configure backup. This way, I can create backups after achieving various milestones in server configuration, and, in case I screw up something badly in follow up steps, I can restore the last good backup instead of reloading and reconfiguring everything from the beginning.

Let us first point out the difference between backup and fault tolerance. Sometimes, when you ask a server administrator what kind of backup he or she has configured, you may hear, "Well I have mirroring of the system disk..." Stop right there.

Disk mirroring is a fault tolerance feature. Disk mirroring will allow your system to keep going when one of the mirrored hard drives fails, but it will not help you if a virus wipes out your system or an interrupted SQL server installation leaves your registry in disarray; your second hard disk will contain a copy of the system that is screwed up just as badly as the copy on the first disk.

Backup on the other hand is a mechanism that allows you to restore whatever had been backed up to the exact condition it was in when the backup was made.

Various backup utilities are available from different vendors, and Windows Server 2008 R2 comes with powerful built-in backup functionality. In this chapter we will concentrate on the latter.

To evoke the Windows Server Backup management console go to Start – Run..., type *WBADMIN.MSC*, and click the OK button. If you have not yet installed Windows Server Backup, you will see instructions on how to do so.

Windows Server Backup allows you to configure a backup to run automatically on schedule, or run once, manually. When backing up once, you can use the same options as for scheduled backup or use different options. The options include backup configuration and destination. To avoid conflicts or lack of space it is recommended that scheduled backups and manual backups are stored in different locations.

The two types of backup configuration are Full server backup and Custom backup. The Full server backup includes all server data, applications, and system state. The Custom configuration allows you to choose specific volumes and files for backup. When selecting what to backup, the "Bare metal recovery" item allows you to quickly select everything that is required to restore the operating system to running state from complete failure.

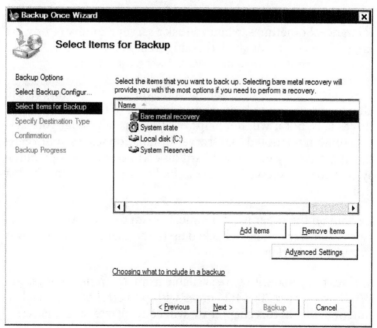

The Full server backup configuration is recommended as it gives you the widest range of recovery options including system state and bare metal recoveries.

Windows Server Backup destinations include hard disks, volumes, DVDs, removable media (except USB flash drives or pen drives), as well as remote shared folders. Scheduling backups to multiple storage disks allows you to rotate between onsite and offsite storage locations.

To restore files, folders, volumes, system state, applications, or application data you can use the Recovery Wizard action in Windows Server Backup management console. To restore the operating system (critical volumes) and full server (all volumes) you will need to run Windows Setup disk or a separate installation of the Windows Recovery Environment. The latter is available by pressing the F8 button when restarting the server, and selecting "Repair Your Computer" from the list of startup options.

Ø4 Name, Domain, and Workgroup Settings

The installation of Windows Server gives your computer an automatically chosen computer name. If you want to change it, the best time to do that is before you start configuring any network services, as some may use the computer name for various default settings.

Click the Start button, then right-click on "Computer", and choose "Properties". The window with basic information about your computer pops up. Click on the "Change settings" link under the "Computer name, domain, and workgroup settings." You will then be presented with "System Properties" dialog box that contains four tabs. Right now we are interested in the "Computer Name" tab, the first tab.

This is where you can give your server a meaningful description, such as "Production Internet Server." You can also click on the "Change..." button to access the "Computer Name/Domain Changes" dialog box.

At the bottom of the dialog box notice the two options in the "Member of" radio button group. These options allow you to configure the computer to be a member of a Windows domain or a workgroup. The difference is as follows. In a Windows domain the user information, including password, is stored centrally in one place. In a workgroup there is no such central repository and each computer relies solely on locally configured user database. Since we are configuring a standalone web server, the Workgroup setting is a better match.

Now take a look at the top portion of the "Computer Name/ Domain Changes" dialog. There is an edit box where we can specify a new name for the computer – we put *MY-SERVER* in there – and a "More..." button. Click the "More..." button to open yet another dialog.

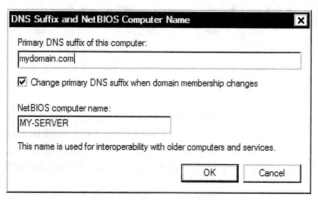

This "DNS Suffix and NetBIOS Computer Name" dialog box allows you to specify the primary DNS suffix of your server and displays the NetBIOS computer name.

The NetBIOS computer name is used for interoperability with Windows NT 4.0 and earlier. Windows 2008 R2 automatically generates a proper NetBIOS name, which it tries to make as close to the computer name as possible. For our purposes, the computer name entered on the previous screen is the important one.

Let us review what the "Primary DNS suffix of this computer" setting does in respect to Internet server configuration.

Participating in great deal of network communications requires identifying computers by name. Sometimes the name is used for informational purposes only, other times the other party is expected to communicate back using the name supplied. The naming standard of the Internet is the Domain Name System (DNS). It is a hierarchical system, where the levels of hierarchy are delimited by dots in the name.

DNS suffixes make your computer name compatible with the DNS. As such, if your computer name is *MY-SERVER*, and your

DNS suffix is *mydomain.com*, together they make up for a full computer name or a fully qualified domain name (FQDN) of *MY-SERVER.mydomain.com*.

Why should we care to have an FQDN for our computer? Well, it depends on what kinds of services you plan on running. If you plan on configuring a fully functional DNS services role, for example, the FQDN is plugged in automatically making the configuration faster and easier.

It is also worth noting that besides the primary DNS suffix, connection-specific DNS suffixes are available in the individual network adapter advanced TCP/IP properties. These are useful if you have your server connected to both Internet and intranet (local TCP/IP network).

Ø5 IP Addresses for Pre-Deployment

Let us say, you decided to place or co-locate your server in a clean, air-conditioned, and secured datacenter of your friendly local Internet services provider (ISP). The ISP dedicated a required number of U spaces in the equipment rack for you. Each U is 1.75"-high, as such the 1U space should be at least 1.75" high, 2U – 3.5", 3U – 5.25", and so on.

The ISP also provided you with the required number of power outlets to feed your server with power backed up by batteries and generators. You also got at least one network connection.

The last but not the least, the ISP gave you a few of the precious public Internet Protocol Version 4 (IPv4) addresses. The pool of never assigned public IPv4 addresses has been exhausted on February 3, 2011. The world is slowly moving towards using newer IP Version 6 (IPv6) Internet addresses. But in our examples we will use the older, classic, IP Version 4.

Throughout the book we will use the following five IP addresses.

    172.31.133.10
    172.31.133.11
    172.31.133.12
    172.31.133.13
    172.31.133.14

Our subnet mask will be: 255.255.255.248

Our gateway address will be: 172.31.133.9

In scripts and configuration options replace these IP addresses with the actual numbers your Internet service provider allocated for your server.

Installing Loopback Adapter

All right, we have our IP addresses, and we plan on hooking them up to various services that our server will run. But, let us say we do not want to do it with the server in the data center, in the rack, and connected to the Internet. How can we pre-configure and test out IP addresses locally, in standalone mode? Loopback adapter will help us.

Loopback adapter is a virtual network card. It emulates real, physical network cards and can substitute for them.

Click the Start button, then right-click on "Computer", and choose "Properties". In the left-top part of the System window, that pops up, click on the "Device Manager" link. In the Device Manager, right click on your server (the top node in the tree view), and choose "Add legacy hardware." The Add Hardware Wizard pops up.

In the Add Hardware Wizard welcome screen click on the "Next" button, and then choose the "Install the hardware that I manually select from a list (Advanced)" option. Click the "Next" button.

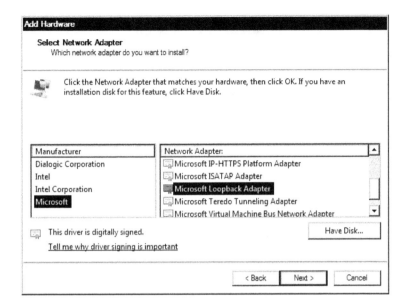

From the list of common hardware types choose "Network adapters" and click "Next." The *Select Network Adapter* screen pops up. From the list of the manufacturers choose "Microsoft," and from the list of network adapters choose "Microsoft Loopback Adapter."

Click the "Next" button, and then the "Next" button again when the Add Hardware Wizard tells you that it is ready to install the Microsoft Loopback Adapter. Click the "Finish" button after the installation is complete.

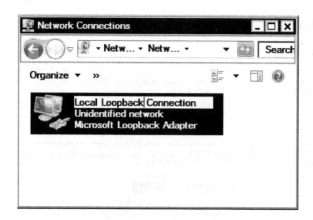

Before leaving the Network Connections screen, let us rename the newly created connection so that we have more clarity when we refer to various network connections in the future. Windows Server 2008 R2 names local network connections as "Local Area Connection," "Local Area Connection 1," "Local Area Connection 2," and so on. Find the newly created connection, right click on it, select "Rename," and change the text to "Local Loopback Connection," which will be our new loopback connection's name.

Adding "Skip as Source" IPs

We have five IP addresses for our server, and we will configure various services listening and responding on these addresses. But what happens when our server wants to communicate with the outside world? Which IP address will the connections originate from? Some applications have built-in knowledge of network topology, but the majority just binds to the TCP/IP stack without caring which source address is used.

In cases where a source IP is not specified Windows Server 2008 R2 uses the target IP address to lookup the best network adapter in the IP routing table, and then applies special logic, which is influenced by preferences of the same address, scope, avoidance of depreciated addresses, preference of outgoing interfaces, and the longest matching high order bits of the network gateway or destination. This logic is used to select an IP address from the entire source IPs set configured for the chosen adapter.

In our example we want to control the source IP. We want the server to use one specific IP address for those outbound communications, and we want to skip the rest. Why do we want this? One scenario is when our server needs to send requests to another server that uses IP based filtering. We would have just one fixed IP to deal with.

Another use is for simplifying DNS configuration where remote SMTP servers check our server's source IP address or its PTR records to insure those are in the permitted set for sending emails. Having just one source IP relieves us from the need to configure all the others.

Click the Start button, then right-click on "Network", and choose "Properties". In the left-top part of the Network and Sharing Center window, that pops up, click on the "Change adapter settings" link.

The Network Connections window opens, find the Microsoft Loopback Adapter, right click on it, and select "Properties". This brings up the Local Area Connection Properties dialog box for the Loopback Adapter. In the middle of this dialog box you will see items used by the connection, select the "Internet Protocol Version 4 (TCP/IPv4)" item and click on the "Properties" button. You will see a new dialog box.

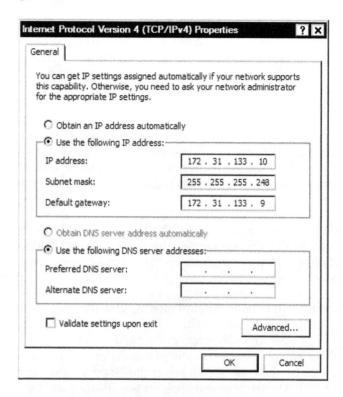

Click the "Use the following IP address:" radio button. And type the IP address that you want to use as source in the "IP address" field. Also populate the "Subnet mask" and "Default gateway" fields with appropriate values.

Now, we could have clicked on the "Advanced" button, and added the reaming IP addresses through the Advanced TCP/IP Settings dialog box, but that dialog box does not have an option of specifying "Skip as Source" properties, so we will add the rest of the IP addresses a different way.

Click the "OK" button on the "Internet Protocol Version 4 (TCP/IPv4) Properties" dialog box to save the changes you made, and then close the "Local Area Connection Properties" window.

To add the remaining four IP addresses we will use the *netsh* utility. This utility can run in simple command line mode, or it can work with script files automating multiple functions. Right now we will just use the netsh utility in command line mode.

Open your server command prompt. It can be accessed from Start – All Programs – Accessories – Command Prompt. And execute the following command (all on one line).

netsh int ipv4 add address "Local Loopback Connection" 172.31.133.11
mask=255.255.255.248 skipassource=true

Replace the IP address and the mask values, with your actual numbers.

Repeat this command for the rest of the addresses, which would be 172.31.133.12, 172.31.133.13, and 172.31.133.14 in our case.

In the command prompt window you do not have to type the whole line again. You can press the keyboard up arrow key, to bring the previously executed command to the front, and edit the command line before running again.

To paste text into the command prompt window you can click on the small icon in the top left corner to call its drop down menu, then select "Edit," and then "Paste." Other options in that sub-menu allow you to mark and copy text from the command prompt window.

To display the list of configured IP addresses use the following command.

netsh int ipv4 show ipaddresses level=verbose

Note the "Skip as Source" flags in the command output. Every time you are not sure if the skip as source properties of an IP address have been overwritten, you can run this command to verify the settings.

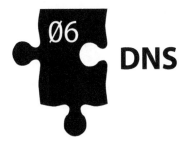

DNS

Our IP addresses are now ready to be bound to, but what about host names? In today's Internet host names are very important, hundreds of web sites for example can run on the same port of the same IP address as the web server differentiates among them by host name. This means we also need to add host name resolution to our server, so that we could test host based network services out before deploying the server.

One way to do this would be by manually editing the hosts file that is located in the *%SystemRoot%\system32\drivers\etc* folder. But since the Windows Web Server 2008 R2 includes a DNS server role that is very easy to use, let us utilize that instead.

Click the Start button, and then select "Administrative Tools – Server Manager." Right click on the "Roles" node under your server in the left panel tree, and select "Add Roles." You will see the "Add Roles Wizard," that we will use now to install DNS Server functionality on our server.

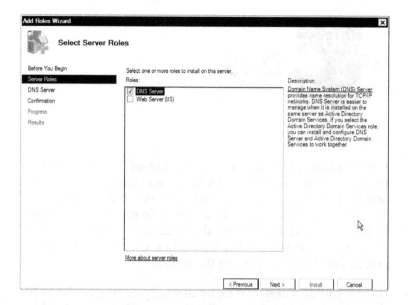

Proceed through the initial screens, and when the "Add Roles Wizard" asks to select one or more roles to install on this server, place a check mark next to the "DNS Server" role in the roles list.

The DNS Server Role does not have any options to configure, so just proceed through to the confirmation screen, and approve installation. After the installation is complete, exit the "Add Roles Wizard."

You will now notice that a new "DNS Server" node has appeared under "Roles" on the "Server Manager" window. Expand that node, then expand the "DNS" node underneath it, and you will see another node for your DNS server, with your server's name.

Before we go any further, let us change one of the default DNS Server settings. By default the newly installed DNS Server role has enabled recursion. Recursion is needed for full featured DNS servers, such as ones deployed by Internet Service Providers, used by clients to resolve the full range of Internet domain names. When such DNS server receives a client request for a domain name it knows nothing about it looks that information up in other DNS servers.

We want our DNS server to answer queries only on domain names we specifically configure. Leaving recursion on when it is not needed is a security risk, which is why we will disable it.

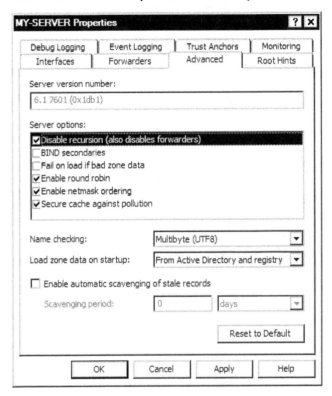

Right click on your DNS Server under "DNS", and select "Properties". Go to the "Advanced" tab, and under "Server options:" place the check mark next to "Disable recursion (also disables forwarders)". Click the "OK" button to save the settings and close the properties screen.

Under your DNS Server on the Server Manager screen notice the "Forward Lookup Zones" and "Reverse Lookup Zones" folders. These are of interest to us, for the basic configuration.

We want to start configuring our DNS Server role by making it resolve our domain name, which in our example is *mydomain. com* to our first IP address, 172.31.133.10.

Make sure "Forward Lookup Zones" folder is selected, then from the "Action" menu select "New Zone..." The "New Zone Wizard" pops up. Click "Next" on the Welcome screen, and you will see a screen that lets you select a type for the new zone.

Secondary zones you will create on a secondary server that copies settings from an already configured primary server. Stub zones, are a special type used in reduced load redundant DNS setups to identify authoritative servers. Right now we want to create a "Primary zone," which is the first option, selected by default.

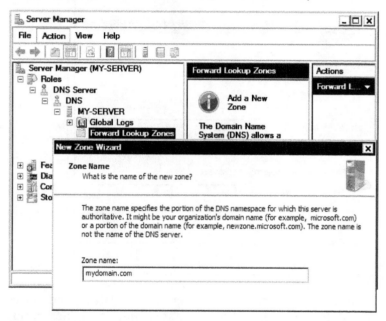

Click "Next" to see the "Zone Name" screen of the New Zone Wizard. Zone name is the highest hierarchy (the least number of dots) name for which this zone is authoritative (queries in which it will answer). Our new zone will be authoritative for the mydomain.com, so that is what we will call our zone.

Put "mydomain.com" in the Zone name edit box and click the "Next" button to proceed to the "Zone File" screen of the New Zone Wizard. If we already had a zone file from another server, we could have specified it here, but since we are creating a new zone file we will just accept the default settings and the default name for the zone file, which is "mydomain.com.dns". Zone files are stored in the *%SystemRoot%\System32\dns* folder.

Click the "Next" button to proceed to the screen which will ask us about Dynamic Update preferences. Dynamic updates allow client computers to register and change their own resources on the DNS server. We do not want dynamic updates, so we will keep the default option of "Do not allow dynamic updates", and click the "Next" button.

After you click the "Finish" button to complete the creation of our new zone file, notice the new zone appearing under the Forward Lookup Zones folder.

We have created our first forward lookup zone; let us now create a reverse lookup zone. Forward and reverse are the two parallel DNS systems used on the Internet. Forward DNS resolves domain names to IP addresses, and reverse DNS does the opposite, it is a special mechanism that returns a host name based on an IP address. It is good practice to keep forward and reverse DNS records synchronized.

Matching forward and reverse DNS entries are required for *Forward-confirmed reverse DNS* (FCrDNS) authentication, often employed to combat spam and phishing.

Right-click on the "Reverse Lookup Zones" folder, and select "New Zone..." Click "Next" on the Welcome screen, accept the "Primary zone" on the Zone Type, click "Next" again, accept "IPv4 Reverse Lookup Zone", and click "Next" once more.

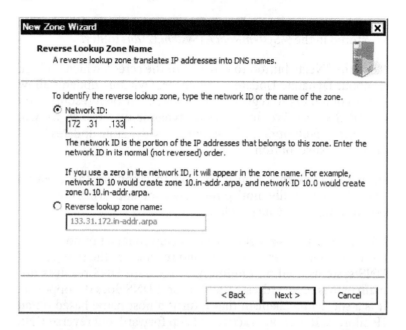

On the "Reverse Lookup Zone Name" screen of the New Zone Wizard you are asked to identify the new zone. You can do that by typing in Network ID, or by specifying the reverse lookup zone name; both accomplish the same thing. We type "172.31.133." in the Network ID fields, which translates to the "133.31.172.in-addr.arpa" reverse lookup zone name.

Click the "Next" button, than accept the default zone file name, click the "Next" button again, accept the default setting of not allowing dynamic updates, click the "Next" button, and click the "Finish" button to complete the wizard.

We are now ready to create the A record and its associate PTR record for our domain. In our example these records establish the relationship between *mydomain.com* domain name and 172.31.133.10 IP address.

Right click on the *mydomain.com,* under "Forward Lookup Zones", under your server, under DNS, under DNS Server, under Roles, in the Server Manager and select the "New Host (A or AAAA)..." menu item. The New Host dialog box pops up.

Leave the Name field blank. The "Fully qualified domain name (FQDN):" field is automatically populated with "*mydomain. com.*" In the "IP address:" field type "172.31.133.10" without quotes, and place the check mark next to "Create associated pointer (PTR) record" option. Click the "Add Host" button to save changes.

You will see a text message, "The host record mydomain.com was successfully created." Then you are returned to the New Host dialog, where you can press the "Done" button to exit.

Let us review what the various fields of the New Host dialog meant. First, as we were creating a record for the *mydomain.com* domain name, we left the Name field blank. If we were creating a record for *www.mydomain.com*, for example, we would have put "www", without quotes, in the Name field.

Next, the "Fully qualified domain name (FQDN):" field is a read-only box that shows us what is the resulting domain name will be for the host we are creating. The trailing dot means that this domain name includes the levels up to the highest, and no resolution of any further parent domain levels should be attempted. In other words this is an absolute domain name, not a domain name relative to the DNS search list.

The IP address is the IP address to which the A record will point. You can have multiple A (or other types of records) point to the same IP address. And since we checked the "Create associated pointer (PTR) record" option, a corresponding PTR record in the Reverse Lookup Zones was also created.

A single PTR record is needed per IP address; you could create multiple, but that is not recommended, unless you have a specific reason for it, as multiple PTR records may confuse some other servers that you server communicates with.

Now that our DNS Server role is running and configured, we need to tell our server's network infrastructure to use our DNS Server for resolutions. We are using the Microsoft Loopback Adapter connection that we earlier named "Local Loopback Connection". Let us adjust that adapter's settings to specify DNS server addresses.

Click the Start button, then right-click on "Network", and choose "Properties". In the left-top part of the Network and Sharing Center window, that pops up, click on the "Change adapter settings" link.

The Network Connections window opens, find the Local Loopback Connection, right click on it, and select "Properties". This brings up the Local Area Connection Properties dialog box for our Loopback Adapter. In the middle of this dialog box you will see items used by the connection, select the "Internet Protocol Version 4 (TCP/IPv4)" item and click on the "Properties" button. You will see the Internet Protocol Version 4 (TCP/IPv4) Properties window.

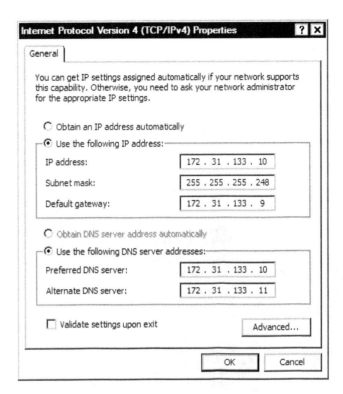

Under "Use the following DNS server addresses:" type one or two IP addresses that correspond to your server. In our example we type 172.31.133.10 and 172.31.133.11. Please note, that here you are using DNS addresses of your own server, not the DNS addresses your internet server provider (ISP) gave you, those you will use on the live network adapter settings. Click the "OK" button to save the changes and exit.

Now let us test how our DNS resolutions work. Open your server command prompt. It can be accessed from Start – All Programs – Accessories – Command Prompt. And execute the *nslookup* command to enter the *nslookup* utility.

At the utility prompt type *mydomain.com* and hit the Enter key. In our example we see the name *mydomain.com* resolve to the 172.31.133.10 address.

Next, at the *nslookup* utility prompt type the following command:

set type=PTR

And hit the Enter key. This command places the utility into reverse DNS resolution mode.

Now type the IP address, which in our case is 172.31.133.10, and hit the Enter key. You should see it resolve to the domain name *mydomain.com.*

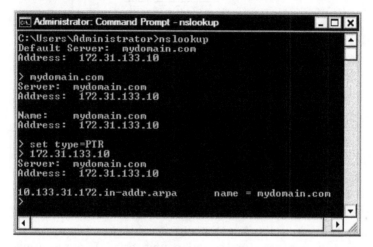

Type "exit" and hit enter to exit the nslookup utility, and then "exit" and hit enter again to exit the Command Prompt.

Our DNS Server is operational and we can use it to set up a full array of DNS records needed to configure and test network services on our computer.

DNS Service on the Internet

The DNS setup we just discussed is sufficient for the purposes of testing environment. You may wish to disable the DNS server role before deploying the server live on the Internet. If you plan to continue using the DNS service for domain name authoritative purposes (that is to resolve DNS records for particular domains) let us review some additional configuration settings.

First and foremost, as we already mentioned, make sure Recursion is disabled in the Advanced DNS Server properties.

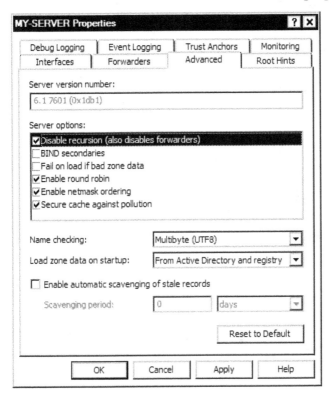

Second, examine zones' properties. Right click on a zone under "Forward Lookup Zones" or "Reverse Lookup Zones" and select "Properties". A couple of settings on the "Start of Authority (SOA)" tab may require adjusting.

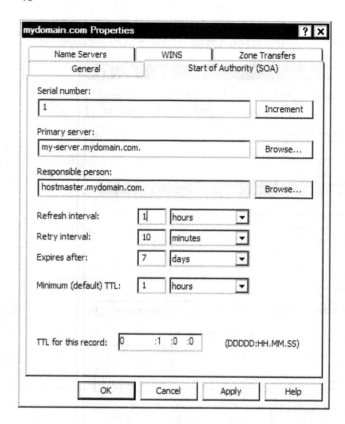

The default settings for "Refresh interval" of 15 minutes and "Expires after" of one day may be considered too aggressive. We usually change these to one hour and seven days respectfully.

Also check the "Primary server" and "Responsive person" settings on the "Start of Authority (SOA)" tab to make sure they are point to the correct records that actually exist on the live DNS servers.

Click the "Apply" button to save the changes.

Now click on the "Name Servers" tab. You may notice that you have only one name server listed with a name based on your computer name, something like "my-server.mydomain.com."

In production Internet environment a domain is expected to be serviced with at least two name servers named like the following.

ns1.mydomain.com.

ns2.mydomain.com.

Adjust the list of authoritative name servers for each of your domains to list appropriate name server fully qualified domain names for primary and all secondary DNS servers. Appropriate A records need to exist; pointing ns1, ns2, and others to their respective DNS server IP addresses.

For production Internet DNS servers, you should have at least two DNS servers in dispersed locations. Configure secondary DNS servers to get updates pushed from the primary DNS server. This can be done through the Zone Transfers and "Notify..." settings in each of the lookup zone properties. When you create lookup zones on secondary servers, create them as secondary zones.

Production Internet DNS servers are expected to link up with upstream DNS servers; plan on communicating with your Internet services provider and Internet domain name provider to set the appropriate records in their DNS servers respectfully. In particular, for reverse DNS to work, you will need to communicate with the provider from whom you obtained the IP addresses to set-up proper reverse lookup delegation. For forward DNS, before setting up authoritative DNS servers they need to be registered (private name server registration) with the registrar of the domain name in which the DNS servers reside.

In the following table you can see a typical set of DNS records for an Internet domain. The domain names in our examples are fictional and used for demonstration purposes only; any match with real Internet domain names is unintentional.

Name	Type	Data	Description
	Start of Authority (SOA)	[23], ns1. mydns.com., hostmaster. mydns.com.	Serial number, primary server, and responsible person
	Name Server (NS)	ns1.mydns. com.	First authoritative server for the domain
	Name Server (NS)	ns2.mydns. com.	Second authoritative server for the domain
	Host (A)	172.31.133.10	IP address for the domain
www	Host (A)	172.31.133.10	IP for the "www." subdomain
*	Alias (CNAME)	mydomain. com.	Alias for unspecified subdomains
	Mail Exchanger (MX)	[10] mymail. com.	Primary mail server
	Mail Exchanger (MX)	[70] reserve. mymail.com.	Secondary mail server
	Text (TXT)	v=spf1 a mx -all	Sender Policy Framework (SPF)

Windows Firewall

Windows Web Server 2008 R2 comes with a software firewall that is enabled by default. The name of this firewall software is Windows Firewall with Advanced Security; we will refer to it as simply Windows Firewall.

A firewall is a layer of protection for your server that in its most important functions blocks access on ports that your server should not be accessed. Windows firewall may also block programs running on your server from accessing the Internet. When enabled, Windows Firewall inspects internet protocol (IP) packets and makes a decision on whether to let them through based on a set of rules. Other functions of Windows Firewall include Connection Security Rules for requiring or bypassing authenticated or encrypted connections and logging ability.

Third Party Mail Server

If you only use built-in functionality of Windows Server you may never have to worry about configuring Windows firewall, as that is done for you automatically when you configure corresponding network services; such as when we installed the DNS Server role, in the previous chapter, the appropriate set of predefined firewall rules was enabled without our intervention. However, if you install networking software provided by third party vendors, you may have to edit the Windows firewall settings manually.

For example, let us see what firewall rules we need to create after we install third party email server software.

Click the "Start" button, then choose "Administrative Tools – Windows Firewall with Advanced Security" to open the

Windows Firewall management console. In the tree on the left pane under "Windows Firewall with Advanced Security on Local Computer" notice four nodes:

- Inbound Rules
- Outbound Rules
- Connection Security Rules
- Monitoring

In this chapter we will concentrate on the first two.

Inbound Rules instruct the Windows Firewall on whether or not to block IP packets originated outside our server. *Outbound Rules* do the same for the packets our server generates or relays to the outside world.

When sending an IP packet a client may bind to a specific port number, such for example in the Dynamic Host Configuration Protocol (DHCP) clients always use UDP port number 68 to communicate with server's UDP port number 67.

More often though, a client does not care which port number it communicates from, it asks the operating system to assign one automatically for the given connection. These automatically assigned ports that are valid only for the duration of a particular connection are called *ephemeral ports* or *dynamic ports*.

By default the range from which Windows Server 2008 R2 automatically allocates ephemeral ports covers the numbers from 49152 to 65535. To see the various dynamic port range numbers configured on your server execute the following commands from the Command Prompt:

```
netsh int ipv4 show dynamicport tcp
netsh int ipv4 show dynamicport udp
netsh int ipv6 show dynamicport tcp
netsh int ipv6 show dynamicport udp
```

You can use the *netsh* utility to change the ephemeral ports range on your server, but your server normally has no control over ephemeral ports other computers employ to communicate with your server.

The range of port numbers from 49152 to 65535 may also contain *private ports* specifically requested by network software. The other two ranges of port numbers are: 1024 through 49151 for port numbers *registered* by various vendors with Internet Assigned Numbers Authority (IANA) and *well-known ports* with numbers from 0 through 1023.

Widely-used network services run on well-known ports. See Appendix II for a list of well-known and some registered port numbers.

When a network service receives a request on a private, registered, or a well-known port number it may answer on an ephemeral port so that to keep the original port open for other clients.

All this needs to be kept in mind when specifying the remote port numbers for Inbound Rules and local port numbers in Outbound Rules. Oftentimes there is no other way but to set these to "All Ports", especially in the Inbound Rules, to guarantee unrestricted communication.

As for local port number in the Inbound Rules, we know that we need to keep the following TCP port numbers open for our mail server:

- 25 – to receive messages relayed by other SMTP mail servers
- 110 – to receive connections from users accessing their POP3 mailboxes
- 587 – to receive messages submitted by SMTP users

You may need to open additional port numbers specific to your mail server implementation. For example, if your mail server users require Internet Message Access Protocol (IMAP) you are likely to add the TCP port number 143 to the list of open port numbers.

Furthermore the secured version of the Simple Mail Transfer Protocol (SMTP) known as SMTPS may require the use of the port number 465, which is actually now depreciated in favor of the so called STARTTLS protocol that specifies how to upgrade a plain-text protocol to an encrypted connection without requiring separate ports.

Similarly, secured versions of IMAP and Post Office Protocol 3 (POP3) may run on ports 993 and 995 respectfully.

An earlier version of the POP3 protocol, POP2, used the port number 109. It is worthy to keep the port number 109 closed as this port number is often attacked by hackers scanning for vulnerabilities that exist in some mail server software. Do not add the port number 109 to the list of open ports.

The Quick Mail Transfer Protocol (QMTP), an alternative to POP3, uses the TCP and UDP ports number 209.

Let us now go ahead and create the inbound rule. Make sure Inbound Rules node is selected in the left pane of the Windows Firewall with Advanced Security management console. Click on the "New Rule..." link in the Actions pane; the New Inbound Rule Wizard pops up.

The first step of the New Inbound Rule Wizard is to select the type of rule. Your choices are: Program, Port, Predefined, and Custom. Select "Custom" as this option lets you to configure the greatest amount of settings right from the get-go.

The next screen of the wizard asks you if this rule applies to all programs or a specific program. We want this rule to apply only to our mail server, and as such we put our mail server executable with the full path into "This program path:" edit box.

Most mail servers run as a Windows Service, however as long as the program is an executable, and we can specify its full path, we can simply specify it as a program; this setting is good for both programs and programs running as services. On the other hand, if our service was in the form of a dynamically loaded library (DLL) we would have to click the "Customize..." button next to the services and configure it there (use only the service name, no path, when configuring firewall rules through the Services option).

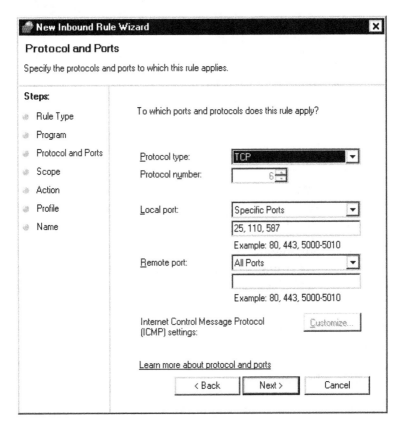

Next is the Protocol and Ports screen. Our mail server uses only TCP protocols. That is what we select in the "Protocol type:" drop down box. If our server needed both TCP and UDP ports open, we would have created a rule for one, and then another rule for the other.

For the "Local port:" we select "Specific Ports", and put the coma separated list of port numbers, "25, 110, 587" (without quotes), meaning that we open the port numbers 25, 110, and 587 on which our mail server will listen for incoming connections.

For the "Remote port:" let us keep the default "All Ports" setting, meaning that we allow TCP packets originating from any port number on the remote computers.

Click the "Next" button to go to the Scope screen that asks to which local and remote IP addresses this rule applies. Keep the default "Any IP address" for both, and click the "Next" button.

On the Action screen, keep the default setting, "Allow the connection", and click the next button.

On the Profile screen keep all three profiles selected, "Domain", "Private", and "Public".

Click the "Next" button to give the rule a name and an optional description. We named our rule "Inbound Mail Server". At the conclusion of the New Inbound Rule Wizard click the "Finish" button to save the new rule.

By default Windows Firewall allows all outbound network traffic. As such we may not need to explicitly create any outbound rules to let our mail server through the firewall. Let us verify that this is the case.

Windows Firewall comes with a set of three profiles: Domain, Private, and Public. A firewall rule can apply to any mix of these three profiles. Any network connection of our server falls into one of the three profiles.

Domain Profile is used for network connections within Windows Domain. Since we configured our server to be a member of a workgroup rather than domain this profile will not come into play in our case. Domain Profile is typically the least restrictive profile.

Private Profile and Public Profile are used for network connections that do not fit the Domain Profile. An administrator can change the type of a network the computer is connected to through the Network and Sharing Center. Designating a network location as "Home network" or "Work network" would enable the Private Profile for connections over this network. The default "Public network" location enables the Public Profile.

Public Profile is typically most restrictive. And the Private Profile is the middle protection setting that is recommended for linking to networks that are not connected directly to the Internet but protected by a security device of some kind.

For network services our computer provides to Internet users it is natural for our rules to include the Public Profile. We also include Private Profile and Domain Profile into any such allow rules as it is expected that anything that is permitted in more restrictive profiles should be permitted in less restrictive profiles as well.

The profiles allow us to specify different restrictions for different types of networks, whether or not inbound and outbound connections are blocked or allowed by default, and we can even turn the whole Windows Firewall on or off for specific profiles.

Click on the highest node in the Windows Firewall with Advanced Security management console. In the middle pane, in the Overview section, you will now see status of the firewall for each of the three profiles.

Windows Firewall is on.

Inbound connections that do not match a rule are blocked.

Outbound connections that do not match a rule are allowed.

"Windows Firewall is on." means that the Windows Firewall is active for this profile, Windows Firewall will examine all the packets on the connections that fit this profile, and make decisions on whether to let the packets through or not.

"Inbound connections that do not match a rule are blocked." means that when other computers initiate network connections to our server, the packets will be blocked by default, unless there is a Windows Firewall rule that specifically allows them. We created such a rule earlier in the chapter.

"Outbound connections that do not match a rule are allowed." means that the packets our server generates when it makes an outbound connection are allowed unless there is a specific rule blocking them. This setting is why we do not need to create a rule allowing our mail server to relay messages to other mail servers, for instance; in our configuration such packets are allowed by default anyway.

The default settings can be changed, and they can differ for each of the three profiles. Click on the "Properties" link on the Actions pane to do so.

Blocking a simple DoS attack

Imagine the following scenario. An attacker tries to gain access to a POP3 mailbox on your server. This attacker sets up a script to brute-force the mailbox by going through all possible password combinations in sequence.

Your mail server software is smart enough to sense the attack and blacklist the offending IP address. Even though POP3 connections from the locked-out IP address are now denied, your mail server is still being bombarded by login attempts. The mail server resources are being consumed, and its log file is polluted. What started as a brute-force attack has now become a Denial of Service (DoS) attack.

In our scenario we are dealing with a simple DoS attack, a DoS attack coming from a single IP host. In contrast to much more vicious distributed denial-of-service attacks (DDoS), in the absence of other mitigating factors, a simple DoS attack is unlikely to cause great harm to our server; nevertheless, before taking time to investigate further, blocking the offending host at the firewall level is recommended.

Create a new Inbound Windows Firewall Rule. For the Rule Type specify "Custom." When the New Inbound Rule Wizard asks you "Which remote IP addresses does this rule apply to?" select "These IP addresses:" radio button, and then click the "Add..." button to add the offending IP Address to the list of remote IP addresses.

The IP Address dialog box is versatile, you can add single IP addresses one at a time, or you can add entire subnets, IP address ranges, and predefined sets of computers.

On the "Action" step of the New Inbound Rule Wizard, select "Block the connection" action. Give the rule a meaningful name and description before finishing with the wizard.

As soon as the new rule is created, you can observe how the flood of bad requests your mail server has to react to stops instantly. We just blocked all incoming communications from the offending IP host at the firewall level, before those have a chance to interact with our email or any other services on the server.

ICMP Ping

You may notice that your server ignores outside ping requests. There is an Inbound Windows Firewall Rule, named, "File and Printer Sharing (Echo Request - ICMPv4-In)". This rule is disabled by default. Enabling this rule enables pings.

Start the Windows Firewall with Advanced Security management console, and open the list of inbound rules. Find the "File and Printer Sharing (Echo Request - ICMPv4-In)" rule, a check mark in a gray circle next to the rule indicates that this rule is disabled. Right-click on the rule and select "Enable Rule" action from the pop-up menu, the circle around the check mark changes to green, indicating that the rule is enabled and Internet Control Message Protocol (ICMP), required for ping to function, is now allowed through the firewall.

Pings are useful for checking and confirming network routing. Other administrators may also ask you to turn pings on while configuring various interconnected services, such as while setting up DNS delegation.

Allowing the ICMP through the firewall carries some security risk. It makes the server vulnerable to such attacks as ping flood. Therefore, it is a good idea to put the rule back in the disabled state once you no longer need the pings on.

Ø8 IIS and Apache

Internet Information Services (IIS) is the name of web server software that is included with Windows Server 2008 R2. IIS is powerful, easy to use, and enjoys highest levels of integration with the operating system. Apache is the name of another web server software suite. Apache is available for wide variety of operating systems and is extremely popular.

A great deal of web sites can run on either IIS or Apache without any modifications. Many can be easily adapted from one web server to another. Some web sites require a particular web server and making them run on another is not easy. Fortunately we can install both IIS and Apache on our server. This way, web sites requiring Apache can run on Apache, and the rest can run on IIS.

It is unlikely that we need Apache to run static web sites. Chances are we will be dealing with interactive web applications serving dynamic data. Such applications are built for various sets of software that provide logic and storage subsystems combined with web serving technology running under an operating system. The name of such a set of software is *stack*.

Dynamic web sites that require Apache are routinely built to take advantage of the so called LAMP stack.

LAMP stands for Linux, Apache, MySQL, and PHP.

- Linux – is the name of an operating system. Linux is a very popular operating system for Internet servers
- Apache – is web server software
- MySQL – is a relational database management system (RDBMS) used to store web sites' data
- PHP – is a scripting language used to implement dynamic web sites' logic

Note that MySQL and PHP do not require Apache. IIS web server software can be configured to run PHP scripting language, and many web applications built for PHP and MySQL can be easily configured to run on ether Apache or IIS with full support from the application vendors.

Still, some web applications rely on features exclusive to Apache and modifying them to run on IIS may be undesirable.

Let us see what we can do to configure our Windows 2008 R2 based server to run web sites built for LAMP.

Installing Apache, MySQL, and PHP

One way to install Apache, MySQL, and PHP on your server is by installing them individually. You can download and install binaries, or you can go as far as getting the source code for each of the products and then compiling it yourself. Either way, you will learn a lot about the products and the configuration options.

For those wishing to take a more express approach, installations that bundle Apache, MySQL, PHP, and, often, additional software in one package exist. A few of these at the time of writing include – in alphabetical order:

- *AMPPS* by Softaculous Ltd.
- *EasyPHP* by Laurent Abbal et al.
- *Uniform Server* by Triple O, LLC
- *VertrigoServ* by Dariusz Handzlik
- *WampDeveloper* by DeveloperSide.NET
- *WampServer* by Romain Bourdon and Alter Way
- *XAMPP* by Apache Friends
- *Zend Server* by Zend Technologies Ltd.

My current favorite out of this list is Zend Server, which is available in free and paid versions, for multiple platforms, including Windows Server.

It is recommended that you have an optimizer in your production PHP installation. The list of optimization products for PHP contains APC by Rasmus Lerdorf, Gopal Vijayaraghavan, Xinchen Hui, et al.; eAccelerator by Dmitry Stogov, Hans Rakers, et al.; PhpExpress by Nusphere Corp.; and XCache by mOo. Zend Server comes bundled with Zend Optimizer+, which, like other optimizers, works by caching and adjusting precompiled PHP script bytecode.

Zend Server can be installed to work with IIS; however in our case we are interested in installing the Zend Server with Apache.

If you want MySQL installed together with Zend Server, make sure to choose the Full setup option or the Custom setup option, as in current versions of Zend Server install, MySQL database is among the options requiring separate download. Zend Server install will download appropriate packages for you automatically; you just need to select the options.

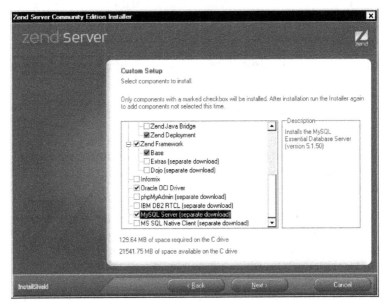

After installing the Zend Server you may be asked to accept the end user license agreement, set the password for accessing the Zend Server administration interface, and supply your e-mail address to opt-in for updates and other notifications.

The Zend Server administration interface is accessible via web browser, and typically runs on the port number 10081 of the localhost. The installation will create a Start menu folder with handy shortcuts.

Adding UNIX Utilities to Windows

Installing Apache, PHP, and MySQL made your Windows Server capable of running the majority of web applications designed for Linux web servers. Still, some of these applications rely on utilities found in Linux that do not exist in a default Windows installation.

For example a web application may have to operate with compressed files. Zip files are no problem, since Windows Server 2008 R2 natively supports zip files, but the web application may also expect, say, .tar.gz files, files assembled into UNIX format tar archive and then compressed using GNU zip algorithm.

Nether tar or gzip/gunzip utilities are available in Windows by default, but you can install them either individually or as a part of a package of the popular UNIX utilities ported to Windows.

One such popular package is UnxUtils by Karl M. Syring.

Usually it is sufficient to put the needed utilities in a folder, and then add the folder to the system PATH variable. Try running the utilities to make sure you included all required libraries and executable files.

Another utility that is familiar to Linux and other UNIX systems administrators is *dig*. Dig is an analog to the Windows *nslookup* utility. If you have to communicate with administrators more familiar with dig, you may wish to have dig on your server.

Arguably dig does some things better than nslookup. For instance, with dig you can diagnose PTR records by performing reverse DNS trace. Try the following command.

```
dig -x 172.31.133.10 +trace
```

Replace 172.31.133.10 with an actual IP address. This displays reverse DNS trace where you can see what kind of reverse DNS records exist, and drill down delegation levels. If you are having problems with PTR records for your IPs, reverse DNS trace may quickly point out the misconfigured DNS server.

The dig utility comes as a part of the BIND DNS server software. You do not have to install the whole BIND server. Simply download the latest stable release of BIND for Windows, and then copy the dig.exe out of the package into a directory on your server. Besides the dig.exe file you will need to copy a few of the supporting dynamically linked library (DLL) files.

The exact files needed may vary from one version to the next, simply run the dig.exe, and it will tell you which DLLs are missing. If you do not already have one installed on your system, you may also get a prompt to install Microsoft Visual C++ Redistributable Package. This package is usually included with the BIND for Windows installation files, or you can get the latest version on the web from Microsoft Download Center.

Installing IIS Role

Installing Internet Information Services (IIS) is as easy as enabling the IIS Role.

Launch the Server Manager, and, if the IIS Role is not already enabled, click the "Add Roles" link.

Put the check mark next to the "Web Server (IIS)" on the "Select Server Roles" window of the Add Roles Wizard.

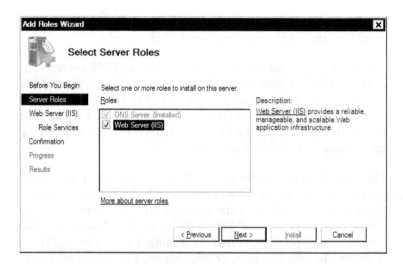

While installing the role, on the "Select Role Services" screen you will be given a chance to choose which IIS features to enable. Some will be already selected, and you can unselect the ones you know you will not need. Such as, if you know that you will never need to list contents of file folders through the IIS, you can unselect the "Directory Browsing" services under "Common HTTP Features."

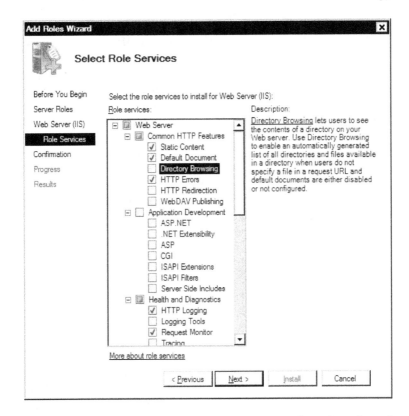

A great deal of the available IIS Role Services will not be selected by default. You can select the ones you know you will need now or you can continue with installation and get back to add more role services at a later date.

Running IIS and Apache Side-by-side

Once you installed Apache and IIS you have two web server systems eager to serve hypertext transfer protocol (HTTP) requests sent to your server.

Specific TCP IP ports are used to serve HTTP requests:

- Port 80 – main HTTP port
- Port 443 – HTTP Secure (HTTPS)
- Port 8080 – HTTP alternate (HTTP-ALT)

Only one web server can answer to requests on a given port of an IP address. If your computer has only one IP address and you wish to run more than one web server on it, you may have to bind different web servers to different port numbers (in that case requesting clients would have to explicitly request non-standard port numbers), or proxy requests through one web server to another.

In our case we have multiple IP addresses. We will dedicate one of the IP addresses to the Apache web server, and we will tell the IIS web server to listen on other specific IP addresses. In our example the IP addresses allocation will look like follows. Adjust your configuration to reflect the actual IP address you received from your internet services provider.

127.0.0.0	– IIS
172.31.133.10	– IIS
172.31.133.11	– Apache
172.31.133.12	– IIS
172.31.133.13	– IIS
172.31.133.14	– IIS

Notice the first address on the list, 127.0.0.0; it is a special loopback network address normally associated with the *localhost* host name. Network applications running on the same computer can use this address and hostname as the means of connection to *this computer*, the computer the applications are running on. In our example we are going to give HTTP processing on this address to IIS.

When you have both IIS and Apache installed on your computer with default settings, IIS binds to all available IP addresses, and when you try to start Apache, you will get the "The requested operation has failed!" error message.

Launch the Event Viewer and go to the Application event log under Windows Logs. There you are likely to see the error message like the following.

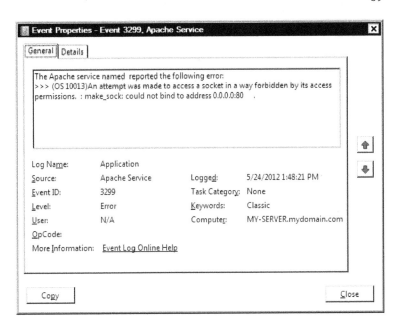

We see that Apache was trying to bind to the port 80 (the number after the colon indicates port number) of all available IP addresses (0.0.0.0 is shorthand for any and all available IP addresses, when used in configuration options).

Let us find the main Apache configuration file. The file name is *httpd.conf* and it is located in the *conf* subfolder under the Apache package main program folder. If you installed Apache as a part of Zend server, your Apache configuration location can be similar to the following.

%PROGRAMFILES(X86)%\Zend\Apache2\conf

Open the httpd.conf file and scroll down to the *Listen* directive.

```
#
# Listen: Allows you to bind Apache to specific IP addresses and/or
# ports, instead of the default. See also the <VirtualHost>
# directive.
#
# Change this to listen on specific IP addresses as shown below to
# prevent Apache from glomming onto all bound IP addresses.
#
```

```
#Listen 12.34.56.78: 80
Listen 80
#
```

The lines in the Apache configuration file that start with the pound symbol ("#") are comments, these lines contain instructions, useful information, and any notes you may want to place in the file. The lines that do not start with the pound symbol are the actual configuration settings. As you see, by default Apache wants to bind to the port 80 on all available IP addresses.

Change the Apache configuration settings Listen directive, as per instructions. Instead of

> *Listen 80*

We will have

> *Listen 172.31.133.11:80*

This instructs Apache to listen on the port 80 of the 172.31.133.11 IP address. You can use multiple Listen directives on separate lines to bind Apache to more than one port or IP address, if desired.

Save and close the httpd.conf file.

Now let us see how to configure binding options for the IIS web server. First, stop the IIS service. You can do that by running the following command from the command prompt.

```
net stop WAS
```

Or you can use the *Stop* action of the IIS Manager.

When you installed the IIS Server Role, the new http context became available in the netsh configuration utility. If you go to the command prompt and execute the following command.

```
netsh http show iplisten
```

You will see the list of the IP addresses on which IIS listens for requests. If you see a blank list that means IIS listens on all available IP addresses.

In the command prompt execute the following commands, one at a time, to add the specific IP addresses to the IIS web server listen list.

netsh http add iplisten ipaddress=127.0.0.0
netsh http add iplisten ipaddress=172.31.133.10
netsh http add iplisten ipaddress=172.31.133.12
netsh http add iplisten ipaddress=172.31.133.13
netsh http add iplisten ipaddress=172.31.133.14

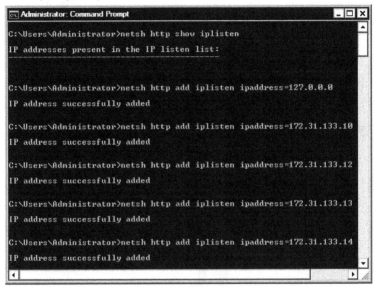

Start the IIS web server using the *Start* action of the IIS Manager, or the following command prompt command.

net start W3SVC

Now you can start the Apache web server; you can do that using the Apache notification icon taskbar shortcut. Apache service by default is configured to start automatically, as such you do not normally need to start it manually each time you restart the computer.

If everything is configured correctly, you now should have both Apache and IIS running side-by-side. Let us open Internet Explorer web browser, type the IP address we associated with Apache web server into the web browser's address bar, and hit "Enter."

Then do the same with one of the IP addresses we associated with IIS.

As you see, default web sites pre-configured with web servers load into the browser window. How to make IIS and Apache serve our own web sites we will discuss in the next section.

Virtual Hosting

We set up web serving software on our computer; let us now see what we need to do to make this software serve our web sites.

In our example we want to configure four web sites associated with the following domain names. The domain names used here are fictional; any matching with real domains on the Internet is coincidental and unintentional. We use these names strictly for demonstration. In your live web server, connected to the Internet, use actual domain names assigned to you by an accredited domain registrar.

www.my-first-iis-site.com – 172.31.133.12

www.my-second-iis-site.com – 172.31.133.12

www.my-first-apache-site.com – 172.31.133.11

www.my-second-apache-site.com – 172.31.133.11

IIS web server on our computer will host the first two web sites, and Apache web server – the other two. The IP addresses we are using here are the ones we configured in the previous section of this chapter.

As you can see, each pair of the web sites will share an IP address. One IP address can be used to serve many web sites; this practice is often referred to as *name-based virtual hosting*, since web server makes the decision on which web site to serve based on the domain name of the web site being requested.

Other virtual hosting types are:

IP-based, where each web site gets its own IP address not shared with any other web site. IP-based virtual hosting is widely used when hosting secured web sites, which we will discuss later in the book.

Port-based, with additional web sites configured to run on nonstandard TCP/IP port numbers. Port-based virtual hosting requires requesting clients to specify the port number in requests they make to the web server. As such, http://www.my-first-iis-site.com:80 and http://www.my-first-iis-site.com:8080 can be two separate web sites, running on the port numbers 80 and 8080 respectfully.

Virtual hosting types can combine and intermingle – you can have web sites running on different IP addresses, with different host names, different ports, or any combination of thereof.

The typical location for public web site files on a Windows server is the *%SystemDrive%\Inetpub* folder. In this folder we create the following four subfolders to serve as physical document root folders for each of the four web sites we are configuring.

> my-first-iis-site
> my-second-iis-site
> my-first-apache-site
> my-second-apache-site

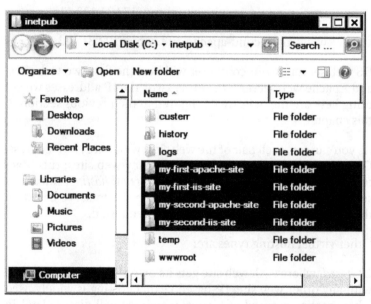

In each of the four folders, create an *index.html* text file with contents like this:

```
<!DOCTYPE html PUBLIC "-//W3C//DTD XHTML 1.0 Strict//EN""http://www.w3.org/TR/
xhtml1/DTD/xhtml1-strict.dtd">
<html xmlns="http://www.w3.org/1999/xhtml">
<head>
<meta http-equiv="Content-Type" content="text/html; charset=utf-8" />
<title>Home Page</title>
</head>
<body>
<h1>Welcome to my-first-iis-site</h1>
</body>
</html>
```

Only, where it says "Welcome to my-first-iis-site," replace the wording to read "Welcome to my-second-iis-site," "Welcome to my-first-apache-site," and "Welcome to my-second-apache-site," in accordance to the folder in which the file is located.

These four hypertext markup language (HTML) files will serve as basic home pages for our web sites. They can be replaced or augmented with more complex content at any time.

The next preparation step is to create forward lookup zones and A-records in our DNS server to point the domain names to specific IP addresses. We discussed how to use the DNS Server Role earlier; please review the DNS chapter of this book for detailed instructions.

Create primary forward lookup zones for each of the four domains we are configuring: my-first-iis-site.com, my-second-iis-site.com, my-first-apache-site.com, and my-second-apache-site.com.

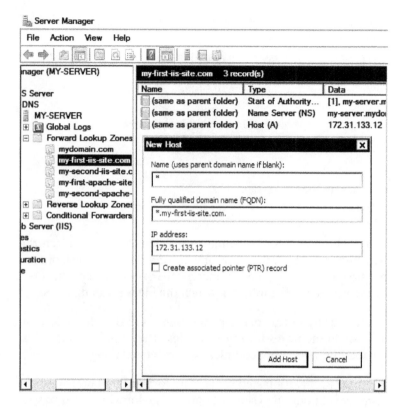

In the forward lookup zones, create A-records pointing to the appropriate IP addresses. In our example the setup is as follows.

> my-first-iis-site.com – A – 172.31.133.12
> *.my-first-iis-site.com – A – 172.31.133.12
>
> my-second-iis-site.com – A – 172.31.133.12
> *.my-second-iis-site.com – A – 172.31.133.12
>
> my-first-apache-site.com – A – 172.31.133.11
> *.my-first-apache-site.com – A – 172.31.133.11
>
> my-second-apache-site.com – A – 172.31.133.11
> *.my-second-apache-site.com – A – 172.31.133.11

The first of each pair of A-records is for resolving requests made to the second level domain name, when the requesting client does not specify the "www" or any other prefix. The other records with the star symbol (*) are for resolving requests to the third level domain names that start with "www" or other words. In our example consider requests to the DNS server to resolve the following domain names.

> my-first-iis-site.com
> www.my-first-iis-site.com
> anything.my-first-iis-site.com

Our DNS server will answer that the IP address for any of these three domains is 172.31.133.12. The A-record without the star will be responsible for the first request resolution, and the A-record with the star will be used to resolve the other two. The star matches "www", "anything," or any other valid third level domain name identification substring.

We already configured our web server software packages to listen on each of these IP addresses, now we need to configure them to discern to which of the web sites requests are made, based on the domain names, and to serve the appropriate sites.

Apache Virtual Hosting

To configure virtual hosting on your Apache Web Server software, first find the Apache configuration file. The file name is *httpd.conf*, and on our computer this file is located in the following folder.

%PROGRAMFILES(X86)%\Zend\Apache2\conf

Your location may vary depending on how you installed the Apache software.

A convenient feature of the Apache configuration infrastructure is the *include* directive that allows including external configuration files instead of polluting the main configuration file with multiple lines of additional configuration options.

In the same folder where the main Apache configuration file is located, let us create a new configuration file named *virtual-hosts.conf*.

At the end of the httpd.conf file add the following line:

```
Include "conf/virtual-hosts.conf"
```

This instructs Apache to read our virtual-hosts.conf file when the configuration is loaded, and to treat anything we put in the virtual-hosts.conf as if it was in the httpd.conf file directly.

You can configure Apache Web Server software in many ways, and the range of the configuration options is vast. Below we review a simple possible configuration for two web sites hosted by Apache. You can use this configuration to get started and expand as needed.

Put the following in the virtual-hosts.conf file.

```
NameVirtualHost 172.31.133.11:80

<VirtualHost 172.31.133.11:80>

        ServerName www.my-first-apache-site.com
        ServerAlias my-first-apache-site.com *.my-first-apache-site.com

        RewriteEngine on
        RewriteCond %{HTTP_HOST} !^www\.my-first-apache-site\.com$ [NC]
        RewriteRule ^(.*)$ http://www.my-first-apache-site.com%{REQUEST_URI}
[R=301,L]


        DocumentRoot "C:/inetpub/my-first-apache-site"

        CustomLog "| bin/rotatelogs.exe logs/www.my-first-apache-site.com.
access.%Y_%m_%d.log 86400 -480" combined
        ErrorLog "| bin/rotatelogs.exe logs/www.my-first-apache-site.com.error.%Y_
%m_%d.log 86400 -480"


        <Directory "C:/inetpub/my-first-apache-site">
                Options -Indexes FollowSymLinks
                AllowOverride AuthConfig FileInfo Limit
                Order allow,deny
                Allow from all
        </Directory>

</VirtualHost>
```

```
<VirtualHost 172.31.133.11:80>

        ServerName www.my-second-apache-site.com
        ServerAlias my-second-apache-site.com *.my-second-apache-site.com

        RewriteEngine on
        RewriteCond %{HTTP_HOST} !^www\.my-second-apache-site\.com$ [NC]
        RewriteRule ^(.*)$ http://www.my-second-apache-site.com%{REQUEST_URI}
[R=301,L]


        DocumentRoot "C:/inetpub/my-second-apache-site"

        CustomLog "| bin/rotatelogs.exe logs/www.my-second-apache-site.com.
access.%Y_%m_%d.log 86400 -480" combined
        ErrorLog "| bin/rotatelogs.exe logs/www.my-second-apache-site.com.error.%Y_
%m_%d.log 86400 -480"

        <Directory "C:/inetpub/my-second-apache-site">
                Options -Indexes FollowSymLinks
                AllowOverride AuthConfig FileInfo
                Order allow,deny
                Allow from all
        </Directory>

</VirtualHost>
```

The *NameVirtualHost* directive, we used, tells Apache that we want it to enable name based virtual hosting on the specified port of the specified IP address (port 80 of the 172.31.133.11 IP address in our example). Port 80 is the standard port for serving http web sites. If you use Apache for name based virtual hosting on multiple IP addresses, repeat the NameVirtualHost directive for each of the IP addresses, and also instruct Apache to listen on each of the needed IP addresses as described in the "Running IIS and Apache Side-by-side" section of this chapter.

Further in the virtual-hosts.conf file you see two *VirtualHost* sections, one for each of the name based virtual hosts we configured. Besides names and locations, the settings between the two are nearly identical. In our example the only difference is the *Limit* option of the *AllowOverride* directive for the first virtual host.

Many Apache web sites and web applications include special *.htaccess* files where instructions to Apache are encoded. Some of these instructions can override settings from the main configuration files. The AllowOverride directive controls which overrides are allowed and which are not. In our example the first virtual host allows overriding of Allow, Deny, and Order host access controlling directives from the *.htaccess* files placed within the web sites. Our second virtual host does not allow such overrides.

The Directory directive tells Apache where the physical location of the virtual host files is, and it hosts other directives that apply to content served from this directory.

Note that instead of simply specifying file names in the CustomLog and ErrorLog directives (which would have created single log files that would have kept on growing) we use the technique called *piping* and pipe logging information to a special log rotation utility that creates a fresh log file, in our case, every day (every 86400 seconds).

The "-480" parameter tells the log rotation utility the offset in minutes from the Greenwich Mean Time when to trigger the creation of the new log files. Adjust this parameter to your time zone, if you want the logs rotated at midnight local time.

Take a look at the three directives bunched together: *RewriteEngine*, *RewriteCond*, and *RewriteRule*. These turn on the Apache URL rewriting engine, set up the condition to activate URL rewriting, and describe how Apache URL rewriting engine should adjust the requested URL when activated. In this case we are using the URL rewriting engine to standardize web site locations.

A web user requesting our web site through his or her web browser can arrive at the web pages in multiple ways. The user can type "www.my-first-apache-site.com" or the user can omit the first "www" and type only "my-first-apache-site.com". We even setup our server so that if the first "www" is replaced with another word, the user would still get to our web site.

As such, requesting "dog.my-first-apache-site.com" or "cat.my-first-apache-site.com" would land the user on the same pages as requesting "www.my-first-apache-site.com." Look in the DNS server settings and in the *ServerName* and *ServerAlias* Apache directives to see all allowed combinations.

Letting URL ambiguity to take place creates a situation where multiple URLs or web addresses are associated with otherwise identical web pages. This can have adverse effects, particularly in the area of search engine optimization (SEO).

Using the three URL rewrite engine directives we examine the URLs requested, and if web users requested anything but "www.my-first-apache-site.com" in the first virtual host configuration or "www.my-second-apache-site.com" in the second virtual host configuration, we fix the URLs up to our preferred format, and automatically redirect the user to the correct URLs.

Last but not the least, let us pay attention to the "Order allow deny" and "Allow from all" directives in the Directory section. Apache has tight security and will not allow serving content from server directories by default. With these directives we allow Apache to serve files from the specific directories to web users.

Familiarize yourself with Apache documentation to learn how to achieve the setup most fitting to your requirements.

After making changes to Apache configuration files Apache needs restarting to load any new settings. You can conveniently restart Apache from the Apache monitor tray icon, from the command line, or from the services control panel.

Test your configuration to make sure every one of the configured Apache web sites loads correctly.

Open Internet Explorer, and request the web sites we just configured to verify that they are being served as expected. If something is not working, you can examine log files for clues.

IIS Virtual Hosting

The control panel central to configuring the IIS web server software is the *Internet Information Services (IIS) Manager*, accessible under *Web Server (IIS)* role in the Roles node of the Server
Manager, from Administrative Tools, or by calling *InetMgr.exe*
directly.

A newly installed IIS role comes pre-configured with a Default
Web Site. This is convenient for checking that IIS is functional.
The Default Web Site binds to the port 80 on all IP addresses IIS
is listening on; before configuring hosting for other web sites on
our IIS server, we can delete or stop the default web site.

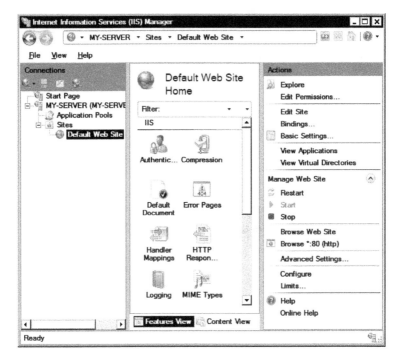

Click on the *Default Web Site* under Sites in the IIS Manager for your server, then in the Actions pane on the right side, click on "Stop" in the Manage Web Site group of commands. This stops the default web site.

Click on "Sites" one level above the Default Web Site on the left panel of the IIS Manager. In the Actions pane, click on the "Add Web Site..." action. The *Add Web Site* dialog pups up.

In the site name edit box type "my-first-iis-site." This is a name we gave the new web site, it does not have to match the domain name or the folder name.

In the physical path, select the folder that we created to serve as the document root for this web site. In our case the folder is as follows. We already put an *index.html* file, in this folder, with some basic text to display to the web site visitors.

C:\inetpub\my-first-iis-site

In the Binding section of the Add Web Site dialog box we need to enter the IP address associated with this web site. You can enter the IP address manually or use the drop down box to select from the IP addresses available. Depending on what updates and hot-fixes you have installed for your copy of Windows 2008 R2, the drop down box may not contain IP addresses configured with the *skipassource* flag. You can still use these IP addresses to serve web sites even if they do not show up on the drop-down box, just type one into the IP address edit box manually.

Last, enter "www.my-first-iis-site.com" into the host name edit box. This enables host based virtual hosting of our web site. We will configure alternative host names in the following steps.

Click the "OK" button to create the new web site with options we specified.

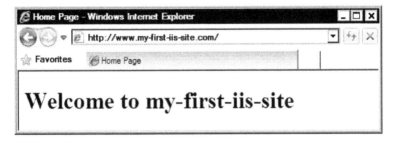

Open Internet Explorer and load www.my-first-iis-site.com, to verify that our newly created web site functions as expected.

Note that if you type "my-first-iis-site.com" into Internet Explorer, the site will not load, as so far the only valid host we specified for our web site is "www.my-first-iis-site.com." Let us now go and add alternative host names for the web site.

Click on *my-first-iis-site* under Sites in the IIS Manager. Then click on "Bindings..." action in the Actions pane. This opens the Site Bindings dialog Box

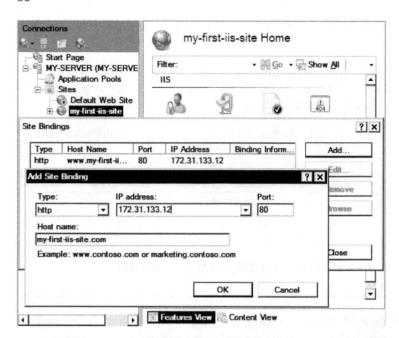

Click on the "Add..." button and add a binding for the same IP address, and the host name "my-first-iis-site.com," without the "www." Click the "OK" button to save the new binding, and then the "Close" button to close the Site Bindings dialog.

Going to "my-first-iis-site.com" will load our web site now, but it will not automatically redirect from "non-www" to the "www" address. When we setup virtual hosts for Apache we accomplished redirection using the URL Rewrite engine. URL Rewrite engine is available for IIS as a separate download that is easy to get through Microsoft Web Platform Installer that we discuss in its own chapter further in the book.

```
┌─────────────────────────────────────────────────────────────┬──────┐
│ Add a rule to redirect to a canonical domain name            │ ? │X │
├─────────────────────────────────────────────────────────────┴──────┤
│                                                                     │
│   Search engines treat Web sites that can be accessed by more than  │
│   one domain name, such as www.contoso.com and contoso.com, as if   │
│   they are two different sites. This affects the page ranking for   │
│   the Web site. Use this rule template to create a redirect rule    │
│   that will enforce the use of a single domain name for the Web     │
│   site.                                                             │
│                                                                     │
│   Select the primary host name:                                     │
│   ┌───────────────────────────────────────────────────────┬───┐    │
│   │ www.my-first-iis-site.com                             │ ▼ │    │
│   └───────────────────────────────────────────────────────┴───┘    │
│                                                                     │
│                            ┌───────────┐   ┌───────────┐            │
│                            │    OK     │   │  Cancel   │            │
│                            └───────────┘   └───────────┘            │
│                                                                     │
└─────────────────────────────────────────────────────────────────────┘
```

Once the URL Rewrite engine is installed, it becomes available in the IIS Manager. You then add a canonical domain name rule from the list of pre-configured URL Rewrite rules. The only parameter you specify is which of the domain names should be the primary host name. All other names will be automatically redirected to the primary host name.

The substitute method that does not require the URL Rewrite engine is to configure a separate IIS web site for all alternative domain names, rather than add those domains to the bindings of the main web site, and then have the secondary web site redirect all requests to the primary web site. *HTTP Redirection* is a service role that can be added to the IIS Server at any time through the Add Role Services wizard in the Server Manager.

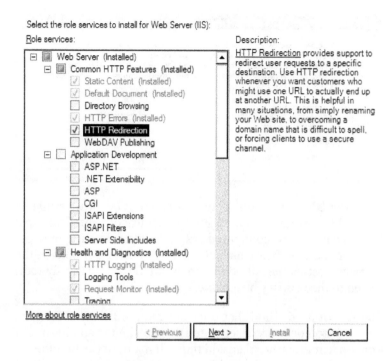

Let us see the substitute method work on our second IIS web site. Add a web site with the following parameters.

> Site name: my-second-iis-site
> Physical path: C:\inetpub\my-second-iis-site
> IP address: 172.31.133.12
> Host name: www.my-second-iis-site.com

Create a new subdirectory *my-second-iis-site-redirect* in the same *inetpub* directory where we created the subdirectories for other web sites.

C:\inetpub\my-second-iis-site-redirect

Note: a separate physical path is needed as IIS configuration settings are stored in *web.config* files in the physical paths. As such web sites with different IIS configurations require separate physical paths.

We do not need *index.html* file in the subdirectory we just created, as we will not be serving anything from it. We just need the subdirectory to store configuration settings.

Now add a new IIS web site with parameters as the following.

Site name: my-second-iis-site-redirect
Physical path: C:\inetpub\my-second-iis-site-redirect
IP address: 172.31.133.12
Host name: my-second-iis-site.com

Edit my-second-iis-site-redirect web site bindings to add two more biddings, so that to have three bindings as follow.

my-second-iis-site.com – 172.31.133.12
dog.my-second-iis-site.com – 172.31.133.12
cat.my-second-iis-site.com – 172.31.133.12

Unfortunately, IIS version 7.5 does not support wildcards for name-based virtual hosting, as such instead of specifying "*.my-second-iis-site.com," we have to explicitly list all valid domain name aliases.

If you have plenty of available IP addresses this deficiency can be eliminated by switching to IP-based virtual hosting. Or, since we have both IIS and Apache installed on our server, you can have Apache handle all non-www subdomains and redirect them to the main domain hosted by IIS.

Once you added all alternative web site bindings to the IIS web site we named *my-second-iis-site-redirect*, double click on "HTTP Redirect" under IIS on the middle pane of the IIS Manager, while making sure my-second-iis-site-redirect home is still selected.

 HTTP Redirect

Use this feature to specify rules for redirecting incoming requests to another file or URL.

☑ Redirect requests to this destination:

```
http://www.my-second-iis-site.com
```

Example: http://www.contoso.com/sales

Redirect Behavior

☐ Redirect all requests to exact destination (instead of relative to destination)

☐ Only redirect requests to content in this directory (not subdirectories)

Status code:

```
Permanent (301)          ▼
```

Put the check mark next to the "Redirect requests to this destination:" option and put *http://www.my-second-iis-site.com* in the edit box beneath. In the "Status code:" drop down box select "Permanent (301)." Click on the "Apply" in the Actions pane to save and activate the settings.

Now try loading my-second-iis-site.com, dog.my-second-iis-site.com, and cat.my-second-iis-site.com in Internet Explorer; they all should redirect to www.my-second-iis-site.com.

Finally, load both *www.my-first-iis-site.com* and *www.my-second-iis-site.com* web sites in Internet Explorer to verify our name virtual hosting on IIS was configured correctly.

Secured Web Sites

When accessing regular HTTP web sites the data travels unprotected, in clear text format. This is fine for public web sites, but unacceptable when serving confidential information. *Hypertext Transfer Protocol Secure (HTTPS)* can be used whenever there is need to encrypt network communication between web servers and clients.

HTTPS works by encapsulating regular HTTP protocol inside Transport Layer Security or Secure Sockets Layer (TLS/SSL) cryptographic protocols.

Before client and server can see the HTTP encapsulated inside TLS/SSL there are several handshake messages sent back and forth to establish the secure connection. Since web site host name is part of the HTTP and not part of TLS/SSL, host based virtual hosting cannot be used with HTTPS, as the server would have no idea which web site a client is trying to reach until the secure connection is properly initialized.

The default port number for HTTPS is 443. You may configure port based virtual hosting for secured web sites, however in this case when requesting any HTTPS web site running on a non-default port, clients have to explicitly specify the port number.

It is customary to use IP based virtual hosting for HTTPS web sites; that is reserve an IP address for each secured web site you want to run. At the same time, using an IP address for a secured web site does not preclude you from running other services on other port numbers of that IP address, including one or more non-secured web sites, with host based virtual hosting for the non-secured web sites, if you wish.

To authenticate that communicating hosts are who they claim they are, TLS/SSL uses certificates.

A required step when setting up a secured web site is obtaining a public key certificate from a certificate authority. You can be your own certificate authority and issue your own certificates. Web browsers come pre-loaded with lists of known certificate authorities, and if a certificate of a web site comes from a certificate authority that cannot be traced on the list, the user will be warned before proceeding to the secured web site. As such, if you are setting up a secured Internet web site, you may want to acquire your certificate from one of the certificate authorities recognized by popular web browsers without displaying warnings.

Please decide what will be the domain name of your secured web site. There is nothing that prevents you from using the same domain name for secured and unsecured web sites. Consequently, if your web site domain name is *www.mydomain.com* you can serve both, unencrypted web site on port 80 and secured web site on port 443.

Consider having a separate domain for the secured web site. Your secured web site domain name could be *secure.mydomain.com*, for example. When the domain name of your secured web site is separate, the risk that clients will load resources from unencrypted web site, instead of secured web site, by mistake, is reduced.

Check with the certificate authority you plan getting your certificate from for details; the common provisions are as follows. When purchasing a certificate for mydomain.com, the certificate authority will generally give you a certificate that is valid for both mydomain.com and www.mydomain.com.

If you need a certificate that is good for any subdomain of a particular level – such as dog.mydomain.com, cat.mydomain.com, or anything.mydomain.com – you can purchase a so-called wildcard certificate for *.mydomain.com. However, wildcards cannot be used with *Extended Validation (EV)* certificates.

EV certificates carry additional information that helps to establish legal identity of the certified web sites. When a user visits a web site secured with a valid EV certificate modern web browsers provide some kind of additional indication, such as truing the address bar green.

Let us go ahead and configure a secured web site on IIS. In our example, we want to host the secured web site using the domain name *secure.mydomain.com*. Substitute you actual registered domain name.

We will designate the IP address 172.31.133.13 for our secured web site. Go ahead and add an A-record to the mydomain.com forward lookup zone, so that secure.mydomain.com points to 172.31.133.13.

Open the IIS Manager, and click on your server home node in the connections pane on the left. In the features view in the middle, find and double click on the "Server Certificates" feature.

Once the Server Certificates screen activates, click on the "Create Certificate Request..." action in the actions panel on the right. This brings up the Request Certificate dialog box.

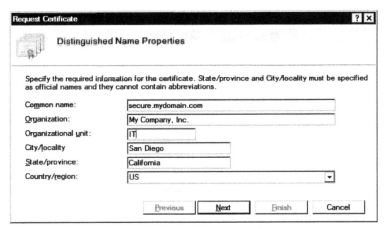

Double check the accuracy of the information you entered, and click the "Next" button to go to the Cryptographic Service Provider Properties screen.

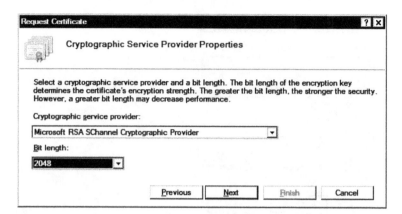

The Ron Rivest, Adi Shamir, and Leonard Adleman (RSA) algorithm, 2048 bits is a good contemporary option supported by most modern clients. Adjust these settings to meet any specific requirements you may have. The bit length refers to the size of the cryptographic key used to encrypt communications. In general, longer keys provide stronger encryption.

Click the "Next" button to go to the screen that lets you specify a file name for the certificate request.

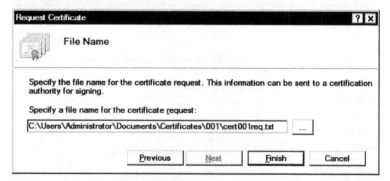

Once you click the "Finish" button, the certificate request file is ready. You can take the certificate request file and upload it to the certificate authority, or paste the contents of the certificate request file in its entirety into an online form, if one is provided by your chosen certificate authority for ordering new certificates.

Once your new certificate is ready, you will generally get it from the certificate authority in a form of a file with "cer" or "crt" extension. If you got a "crt" file, open if first, go the "Details" tab, click on the "Copy to File..." button, which brings up a certificate export wizard. Choose the options "No, do not export the private key" and "Base-64 encoded X.509 (.CER)" and then save the certificate into a "cer" file.

Go back to the "Server Certificates" feature of the IIS Manager, and click on "Complete Certificate Request..." in the Actions pane.

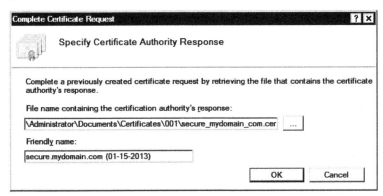

Navigate to the "cer" certificate file in the file name edit box, and in the friendly name edit box put a name that will be used when displaying available certificates. Friendly name is not required, but it is handy for distinguishing between different certificates when you use multiple.

Once you click the "OK" button, the certificate is imported and is ready to use by the IIS.

Create a new subfolder in the inetpub folder to serve as the physical document root for our secured web site.

C:\inetpub\secure-mydomain

In that folder, create an *index.html* text file with the following content.

```
<!DOCTYPE html PUBLIC "-//W3C//DTD XHTML 1.0 Strict//EN" "http://www.w3.org/TR/
xhtml1/DTD/xhtml1-strict.dtd">
<html xmlns="http://www.w3.org/1999/xhtml">
<head>
```

```
<meta http-equiv="Content-Type" content="text/html; charset=utf-8" />
<title>Home Page</title>
</head>
<body>
<h1>Welcome to secure.mydomain.com</h1>
</body>
</html>
```

Now, click on "Sites" in the IIS Manager, and create a new web site with the following parameters.

> Site name: secure-mydomain
> Physical path: C:\inetpub\secure-mydomain
> Type: https
> IP address: 172.31.133.13

In the SSL certificate drop down box select the certificate we just imported.

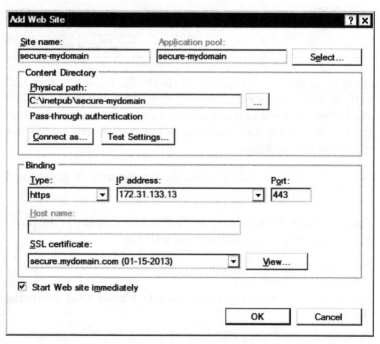

Click the "OK" button to save and start the new web site.

Finally, open Internet Explorer and go to *https://secure.mydomain.com/* to verify that the secured web site loads as expected.

Make sure to renew any certificates, you use, before they expire. To start certificate renewal from the "Server Certificates" feature of the IIS Manager, select an active certificate on the list of server certificates, and click "Renew..." on the Actions pane. The certificate authority, that sold you the certificate, may also have specific renewal instructions for you.

Keep in mind that you can employ a certificate in more than one application. For example, if you have mail software running on your server, and that software supports transport layer security, you can import or select from store that same certificate you are using on the web server to also use it in the mail server software; configure the mail server to answer on the same secure domain (secure.mydomain.com in our case), and instruct your mail clients to connect to the secure domain with secure protocols.

You can also have the same certificate securing your remote desktop sessions.

Naturally, the more places there are where a certificate is used, the more exposure there is. If such certificate gets compromised, you have to replace it everywhere it was installed.

Ø9 ASP.NET 1.1 on Windows 2ØØ8 R2

ASP.NET is a robust web application framework from Microsoft, arguably the most successful part of the .NET initiative. ASP.NET version 1.1 was the first version of ASP.NET embraced by web developers everywhere. The amount of web applications created for ASP.NET 1.1 is massive.

Windows 2008 R2 does not officially support ASP.NET 1.1.

If you are migrating to Windows 2008 R2, and stumble upon ASP.NET 1.1 applications or services your server needs to run, you have a few choices:

· You can contact the application vendor to see if a newer version is available.

· Many ASP.NET 1.1 applications will happily run in an ASP.NET 2.Ø application pool. Try your application; just make sure to run applications that target different versions of ASP.NET in different pools.

· If you have the source code, you can attempt to recompile the application against a newer version of the framework. Visual Web Developer component of Microsoft Visual Studio features a Conversion Wizard that may help you retargeting older web applications or services from ASP.NET 1.1 to a newer version.

· Even though it is not officially supported, you can install ASP.NET 1.1 on your server.

Warning: while the author has tested the last option, there is no guarantee that it will work with your particular web applications.

And when it works, future updates to the operating system or server software may break the compatibility at any time.

If you are determined to install ASP.NET 1.1 on Windows 2008 R2, here are the steps we have tested.

ASP.NET 1.1 communicates with IIS using the older style metabase, rather than the new configuration of IIS version 7 and later. Use the *Add Role Services* wizard of Server Manager to install IIS 6 Metabase Compatibility:

Management Tools

    IIS 6 Management Compatibility

        IIS 6 Metabase Compatibility

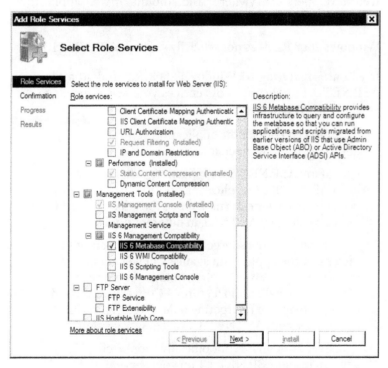

At the same time we will need some options under Application Development, make sure those are enabled as well:

Web Server

        Application Development

             ASP.NET

             .NET Extensibility

             ISAPI Extensions

             ISAPI Filters

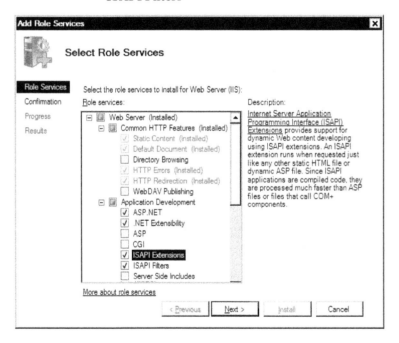

Create an IIS web site under which your ASP.NET 1.1 application will run. We named our web site *aspnet11test*.

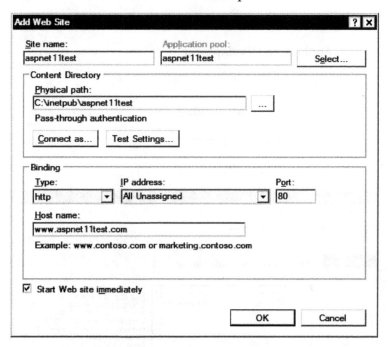

Obtain the following installation packages, available from Microsoft Download Center:

· Microsoft .NET Framework Version 1.1 Redistributable Package (dotnetfx.exe)

· Microsoft .NET Framework 1.1 Service Pack 1 (NDP1.1sp1-KB867460-X86.exe)

· ASP.NET Security Update for Microsoft .NET Framework 1.1 Service Pack 1 (NDP1.1sp1-KB886903-X86.exe)

Install these packages on your server, in order. You will get incompatibility warnings.

Restart the server after installing all three packages.

ASP.NET 1.1 applications store their settings in *web.config* files. Newer versions of the IIS web server software stores its own configuration settings in *web.config* files as well. When ASP.NET 1.1 applications encounter sections of *web.config* files generated by the IIS, errors may result. Let us make a change in the settings of ASP.NET 1.1 to teach it ignoring IIS configuration sections.

Find and open the ASP.NET 1.1 *machine.config* file. Its normal location is:

%windir%\Microsoft.NET\Framework\v1.1.4322
config\machine.config

Just before the </configSections> closing tag add the following line.

```
<section name="system.webServer" type="System.Configuration.IgnoreSectionHandler,
System, Version=1.0.5000.0, Culture=neutral, PublicKeyToken=b77a5c561934e089" />
```

This will prevent ASP.NET 1.1 from getting confused by the new way IIS server stores configuration settings.

Now install your ASP.NET 1.1 application under the IIS web site you prepared. Web applications may be deployed just by copying files, or come in form of installation packages. In our example we are using an ASP.NET 1.1 application called Web File Manager, featuring its own install.

Our sample application install automatically created a web application called *WebFileManager* under our *aspnet11test* web site we specified. Depending on how you are installing your ASP.NET 1.1 application, you may need to manually create the web application. You can do that by right clicking on the application folder in the IIS Manager, and selecting "Convert to Application."

At this point you can try accessing your web application from Internet Explorer. ASP.NET is a resilient platform and, depending on what resources the web application calls for, the application may already work, and no further configuration will be necessary. If not, continue.

Select your server in the IIS, the node above *Sites* in IIS Manager, and locate the "ISAPI and CGI Restrictions" feature.

ISAPI and CGI Restrictions

Activate *ISAPI and CGI Restrictions* and in the list of restrictions change the option for "ASP.NET v1.1.4322" from *Not Allowed* to *Allowed*. If you do not see the ASP.NET v1.1.4322 aspnet_isapi. dll on the list, then add it manually, using the "Add..." action.

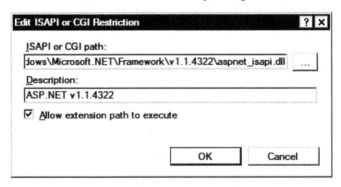

The full path to the ASP.NET v1.1.4322 aspnet_isapi.dll is normally *C:\Windows\Microsoft.NET\Framework\v1.1.4322\ aspnet_isapi.dll*.

In order to make ASP.NET 1.1 show up in the list of available application pools, open the command prompt, and execute the following command (all on one line).

```
MKLINK /d %windir%\Microsoft.NET\Framework64\v1.1.4322 %windir%\Microsoft.
NET\Framework\v1.1.4322
```

Now let us create an application pool for our ASP.NET 1.1 application. In the IIS manager go to "Application Pools" under your server top node.

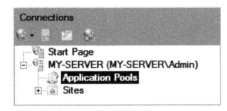

In the Actions pane click on "Add Application Pool..."

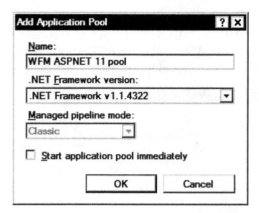

Give the new application pool a name; we named ours "WFM ASPNET 11 pool." From the .NET Framework version drop down box select ".NET Framework v.1.1.4322." Leave the Managed pipeline mode setting on "Classic," and uncheck the "Start application pool immediately" check box. Click the OK, button to create the pool.

Now, right click on the newly created application pool, and go to the "Advanced Settings..."

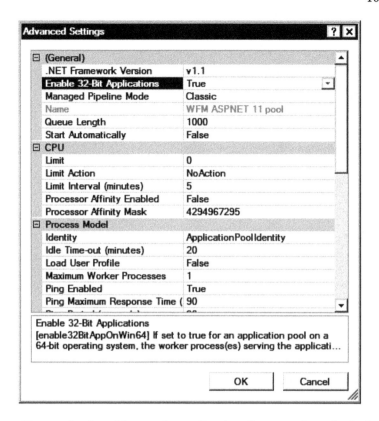

Change the "Enable 32-Bit Applications" setting from "False" to "True." Click OK to save the application pool settings.

Right click on the application pool again, and click "Start" to start it.

Now let us go back to the site we are working on, under "Sites." Select the ASP.NET 1.1 application in the left hand side tree under the site. Next, in the Actions, under "Manage Application" click on "Advanced Settings..."

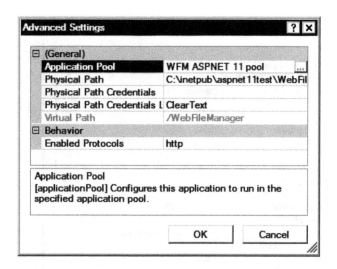

Change the "Application Pool" property to the application pool we just created. Click the OK button to save the changes.

Now everything should be working. Open Internet Explorer and browse to your web application.

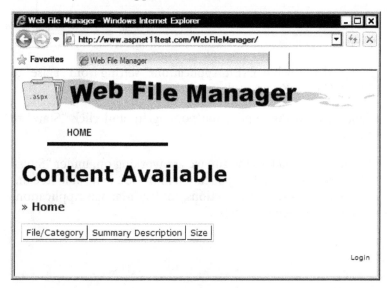

If something is not right, examine log files and event viewer for messages.

10 Indexing Services for IIS

In the days of Internet at the turn of the century, it was customary for every self-respecting web site to feature a search box. Virtually any professionally designed web site template included a placeholder, with an edit box for visitors to put a search term, and a button (often with a magnifying glass picture) to activate the search.

In order to make the search work, Web sites running on Unix-based platforms often relied on additional software, software such as *ht://Dig* by Andrew Scherpbier of, then, San Diego State University. Web platforms based on Windows already had included all the pieces required to expose search functionality to web site visitors, utilizing the file indexing services of the operating system. Windows 2008 R2 Web Server continues to provide this functionality for those who need it.

Before implementing Indexing Services for your web site please consider other options. Visitors browsing for information in this day and age are conditioned to use Internet search engines, with Google being the most prominent one. As such, people coming from search engines can be expected to already land on the web page most relevant to their search term.

If additional searching is necessary, then ask yourself, why. If this is because the visitors are searching for a product in your online shop, then you need to direct them to the product search. And the product search is much better implemented as a well-tuned part of your online store application rather than a search on indexed static files.

Furthermore, if the amount of your static content is great enough to require indexing, you may benefit from a content management system (CMS). The content management system will not only provide search, but also simplify unified access, enable visitor comments, allow for automatic syndication feeds, as well as bookmarking, social networking, and printing functionality with no manual effort.

Popular content management systems include:

- *DotNetNuke* by DotNetNuke Corporation
- *Drupal* by Dries Buytaert
- *Joomla* by The Joomla Project Team
- *SharePoint* by Microsoft Corporation
- *WordPress* by WordPress Foundation

If, after considering the options, you still find the need to implement search among the static content on the web server, let us examine how to make that happen under Windows 2008 R2.

Launch the Server Manager (ServerManager.msc) and activate the "Features" node in the left pane tree. Click on "Add Features" on the right side.

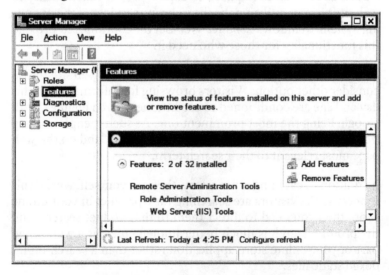

Place a check mark next to the *Indexing Service* feature, and follow installation prompts to activate it on your server.

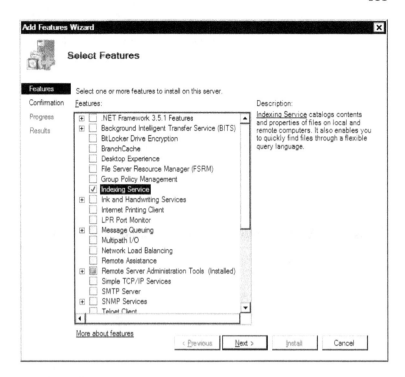

For our experiment with Indexing Services we created an IIS web site with physical folder at the following location.

C:\inetpub\war-and-peace

Our web site name is *war-and-peace*.

Substitute your actual web site and folder when following these instructions. The web site for this example consists of sixteen *html* files containing the famous novel "War and Peace" by author Leo Tolstoy. There is also an *index.html* file with links to the book chapters. We want to add a search box to the *index.html* file to search through the web site content using Indexing Services.

First, open your web site in Internet Explorer and browse through pages, to make sure the web site is running and fully operational.

Using the *Add Role Services* wizard of Server Manager make sure the following role services are enabled in your IIS web server role:

Management Tools

    IIS 6 Management Compatibility

        IIS 6 Metabase Compatibility

        IIS 6 WMI Compatibility

        IIS 6 Scripting Tools

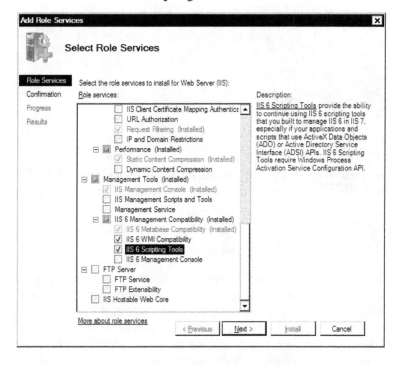

At the same time we will need some options under Application Development, make sure those are enabled as well:

Web Server

    Application Development

        ISAPI Extensions

        ISAPI Filters

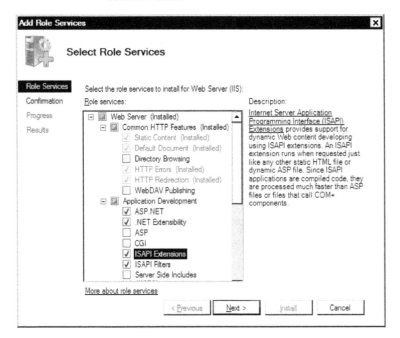

To show the Indexing Services which web resources it is allowed to index we need to set the resources' metabase *ContentIndexed* property to "1." We will do that with command line scripts.

Before executing the scripts find out what is your web site *identification number* (ID). For that, right click on the web site in the IIS Manager; in the pop-up menu go to "Manage Web Sites", and then to "Advanced Settings..."

In the Advanced Settings dialog find the ID field in the General section, and note the ID number. In our example the ID number is "7."

Open command prompt, and change the current directory to %systemdrive%\inetpub\adminscripts.

cd %systemdrive%\inetpub\adminscripts

Now execute the following command.

cscript adsutil.vbs set w3svc/7/root/ContentIndexed 1

Substitute "7" for your actual web site ID number.

If the content you want indexed is not in the root directory, then specify the path after the root. For example if our content was in a virtual directory named VirDirOne, then the command to execute would be as follows.

cscript adsutil.vbs set w3svc/7/root/VirDirOne/ContentIndexed 1

Adjust your command lines as needed for your actual web site ID and content directories you want indexed.

Next, activate the Computer Management Console (Start – Administrative Tools – Computer Management). Under "Services and Applications," in the left hand tree, locate "Indexing Service."

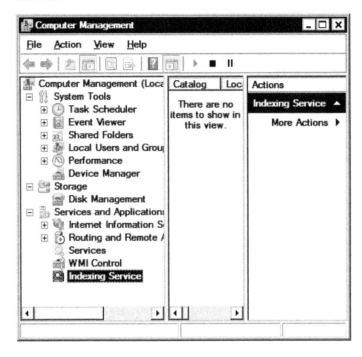

You can also call CIADV.MSC – Indexing Service management console – directly.

In the Indexing Service management console select "New" – "Catalog" from the Action menu.

Choose a name for your catalog and storage location. You will get a warning message: "Catalog will remain offline until the Indexing Service is restarted."

Expand the catalog you just created. You will find two items underneath: "Directories" and "Properties." Right click on "Directories" and choose "New" – "Directory."

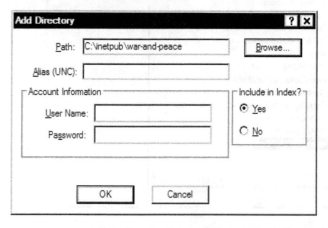

Specify the path to your web site content to be indexed and leave all other fields as is. Click "OK" to save changes.

Right click on the "Indexing Service" in the left hand tree, and select "Stop." Then, right click on your catalog under "Indexing Service," and select "Properies" from the pop-up menu. The catalog properties dialog box pops up with three tabs: "General," "Tracking," and "Generation." Select the "Tracking" tab. In the "WWW Server" drop down box, select the web site for which you are configuring the service.

Then go to the "Generation" tab, uncheck the "Inherit above settings from Service" check box, and check the "Generate abstracts" check box. In the "Maximum size (in characters):" box, you can specify how long the abstracts, the blurbs of text in search results, should be.

Click the "OK" button to save the changes.

Right click on the "Indexing Service" in the left hand tree, and select "Start." Your indexing service is now working. The next step is to build the front end for web site visitors to use the search.

In the web site physical directory, *C:\inetpub\war-and-peace* in our case, create a new subdirectory. Let us name the new subdirectory *SearchIndex*. In this directory create two text files *query. idq* and *query.htx*.

The *query.idq*, the so called *Internet Data Query File*, defies which Indexing Services catalog to query and other parameters. Following is what we have in the *query.idq* file in our example. Lines that begin with the pound sign are comment lines.

```
# [Names]
# The Names section is not required if using default settings.

[Query]

CiCatalog=C:\Catalogs\war-and-peace

# REQUIRED PARAMETERS

CiScope=/
# CiScope is the directory for which results are returned.
# You can specify a subdirectory by including it in the CiScope,
# for example, CiScope=/legis/laws/mgl
# If a file matches the query but is not in a directory beneath
# CiScope, it is not returned in the result set.  (see also CiFlags)

CiColumns=filename,size,rank,characterization,vpath,DocTitle,write
# CiColumns specifies the elements referenced in the .htx files
# when formatting output for each hit.

CiTemplate=/SearchIndex/query.htx
# CiTemplate indicates the .htx file to use for formatting the results
# of the query.

CiRestriction=%Search%
# The CiRestriction is the query.  Here, it's passed in from of the
# form in the .htm file
# (<input type="text" size="45" maxlength="125" name="Search">)
```

OTHER PARAMETERS

CiFlags=DEEP
# Do a recursive search (i.e., all directories under CiScope).
# The opposite is SHALLOW

CiMaxRecordsInResultSet=300
# Do not allow more than 300 total hits in the result set.
# If you want your results page to display a statement such as
# "Page 1 of 10", you need to specify CiMaxRecordsInResultSet

CiMaxRecordsPerPage=10
# Display CiMaxRecordsPerPage hits on each page of output

CiSort=rank[d]
# This is the list of property names to use in sorting the results.
# Append [a] or [d] to the property name to specify ascending or
# descending. Separate keys in multi-key sorts with commas.
# For example, to sort on file write date ascending, then file size
# descending, use CiSort=write[a],filesize[d]

CiLocale=En-US
# Setting CiLocale allows the web master to override the locale sent from
# the browser.
# The locale affects the formatting of dates, times, and numbers. Currency
# is formatted according to the locale of the web server. Locale is also
# used to select the word breaker, and the stop word list.
# If CiLocale is not found in the IDQ file the locale sent by the web
# browser is used. If no locale is send from the browser, the locale of
# the web server is used.
# The web browser sends its locale via the HTTP_ACCEPT_LANGUAGE parameter
CiDialect=1

The *query.htx* file holds a template used to create web pages for displaying search results. The content of our *query.htx* file follows.

```
<!DOCTYPE html PUBLIC "-//W3C//DTD XHTML 1.0 Transitional//EN" "http://www.w3.org/
TR/xhtml1/DTD/xhtml1-transitional.dtd">
<html xmlns="http://www.w3.org/1999/xhtml">
<head>
```

```
<meta http-equiv="Content-Type" content="text/html; charset=utf-8" />
<title>War and Peace Search Results</title>
</head>

<body>
<h1>Search Results</h1>
<h5>
<%if CiMatchedRecordCount eq 0%>
No documents matched the query &quot;<%Search%>&quot;.
<%else%>
Documents <%CiFirstRecordNumber%> to <%CiLastRecordNumber%> (of
<%CiMatchedRecordCount%>) matching the query <i><%Search%></i>.
<%endif%>
</h5>

<!--
   This area formats each of the items found in the search
-->

<%begindetail%>
   <dl compact="compact">
   <dt>
   <%CiCurrentRecordNumber%>.
   <%if DocTitle isempty%><a href="<%EscapeURL
vpath%>"><b><%filename%></b></a>
   <%else%><a href="<%EscapeURL vpath%>"><b><%DocTitle%></b></a>
   <%endif%></dt>
   <dd><b><i>Abstract: </i></b>
   <%characterization%><br />
   <a href="<%EscapeURL vpath%>"><cite>http://<%server_
name%><%vpath%></cite></a><br />

   <%if size eq ""%>
   <cite>(size and time unknown)</cite>
   <%else%>
   <cite>size <%size%> bytes - <%write%> GMT</cite>
   <%endif%>
   </dd></dl>
<%enddetail%>

<!--
```

Include a form so the user can enter a new search query if they are
dissatisfied with the results
-->

New query:
```
<form action="/SearchIndex/query.idq" method="get">
<p><i>New Search:</i><br />
<input type="text" size="45" maxlength="125" name="Search" />
<input type="submit" value="New Search" /><br />
</form>

<!--
This piece makes buttons to retrieve the next and previous set of results
-->

<%if CiContainsFirstRecord eq Ø%>
    <form action="/SearchIndex/query.idq" method="get">
    <input type="hidden" name="CiBookMark" value="<%CiBookMark%>" />
    <input type="hidden" name="CiBookmarkSkipCount" value="-<%EscapeRAW
CiMaxRecordsPerPage%>" />
    <input type="hidden" name="CiMaxRecordsInResultSet" value="<%EscapeRAW
CiMaxRecordsInResultSet%>" />
    <input type="hidden" name="Search" value="<%Search%>" />
    <input type="hidden" name="CiMaxRecordsPerPage" value="<%EscapeRAW
CiMaxRecordsPerPage%>" />
    <input type="submit" value="Previous <%CiMaxRecordsPerPage%> Documents" />
    </form>
<%endif%>
<%if CiContainsLastRecord eq Ø%>
    <form action="/SearchIndex/query.idq" method="get">
    <input type="hidden" name="CiBookMark" value="<%CiBookMark%>" />
    <input type="hidden" name="CiBookmarkSkipCount" value="<%EscapeRAW
CiMaxRecordsPerPage%>" />
    <input type="hidden" name="CiMaxRecordsInResultSet" value="<%EscapeRAW
CiMaxRecordsInResultSet%>" />
    <input type="hidden" name="Search" value="<%Search%>" />
    <input type="hidden" name="CiMaxRecordsPerPage" value="<%EscapeRAW
CiMaxRecordsPerPage%>" />
    <input type="submit" value="Next <%CiRecordsNextPage%> Documents" />
    </form>
<%endif%></h5>
```

```
<p><br />

<!--
   If the query took too long to execute (for example, if too much work
   was required to resolve the query), let the user know
-->

<%if CiQueryTimedOut ne 0%>
</p>
<p>
   <i><b>The query took too long to complete.</b></i><br />
<%endif%>


<!--
   Output a page number and count of pages
-->

<%if CiTotalNumberPages gt 0%>
</p>
<p>
   Page <%CiCurrentPageNumber%> of <%CiTotalNumberPages%>
</p>
<p>
<%endif%>
</p>
<p><a href="/">Home</a></p>
</body>
</html>
```

Now, let us modify the homepage *index.html* file, in the web site
physical root folder, to add a search box. Our *index.html* file will
look like the following.

```
<!DOCTYPE html PUBLIC "-//W3C//DTD XHTML 1.0 Transitional//EN""http://www.w3.org/
TR/xhtml1/DTD/xhtml1-transitional.dtd">
<html xmlns="http://www.w3.org/1999/xhtml">
<head>
<meta http-equiv="Content-Type" content="text/html; charset=utf-8" />
<title>War and Peace Index</title>
</head>
<body>
<h1>War and Peace</h1>
```

```
<h2>By Leo Tolstoy</h2>
<form action="/SearchIndex/query.idq" method="get">
 <p><i>Search for words or phrases on the book:</i><br />
  <input type="text" size="45" maxlength="125" name="Search" />
  <input type="submit" value="Search" />
  <br />
 </p>
</form>
<h3>Index</h3>
<p>Book First: <a href="tvm_1_1.htm">part one</a>, <a href="tvm_1_
2.htm">part two</a>, <a href="tvm_1_3.htm">part three</a></p>
<p>Book Second: <a href="tvm_2_1.htm">part one</a>, <a href="tvm_2_
2.htm">part two</a>, <a href="tvm_2_3.htm">part three</a>, <a href="tvm_2_
4.htm">part four</a>, <a href="tvm_2_5.htm">part five</a></p>
<p>Book Third: <a href="tvm_3_1.htm">part one</a>, <a href="tvm_3_
2.htm">part two</a>, <a href="tvm_3_3.htm">part three</a></p>
<p>Book Fourth: <a href="tvm_4_1.htm">part one</a>, <a href="tvm_4_
2.htm">part two</a>, <a href="tvm_4_3.htm">part three</a>, <a href="tvm_4_
4.htm">part four</a></p>
<p><a href="tvm_eplg.htm">Epilogue</a></p>
</body>
</html>
```

The search box that we added is between the *<form...></form>* tags.

Next, open the IIS Manager and in the left pane tree navigate to the *SearchIndex* folder under the web site we are working on. In the middle pane, in the IIS section, locate the *Handler Mappings* feature.

Double click on *Handler Mappings*, and in the actions pane click on the "**Add Script Map...**" action.

In the *Add Script Map* dialog box put "*" in the "Request path:" edit box (without quotes). Browse to the *idq.dll* in the "Executable:" box. The *idq.dll* is normally located in the *%WINDIR%/System32* folder. And give the script map a meaningful name in the "Name:" edit box. We chose "Indexing Service dll" for the name. Click the "OK" button.

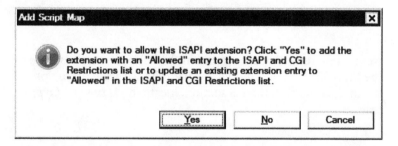

IIS Manager will offer to add the dynamically linked library (dll) to the list of allowed ISAPI extensions. This is needed for the web search to work. Click the "Yes" button to agree.

Open Internet Explorer, and navigate to the web site we have been setting up.

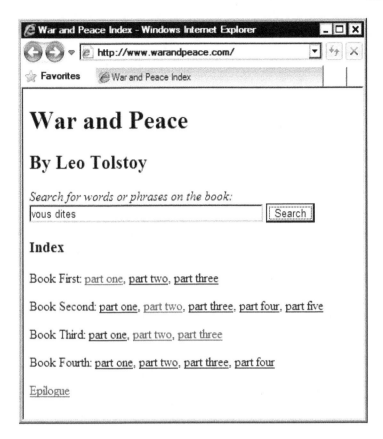

Put a search term in the search edit box, and click the "Search" button. You should get the search results.

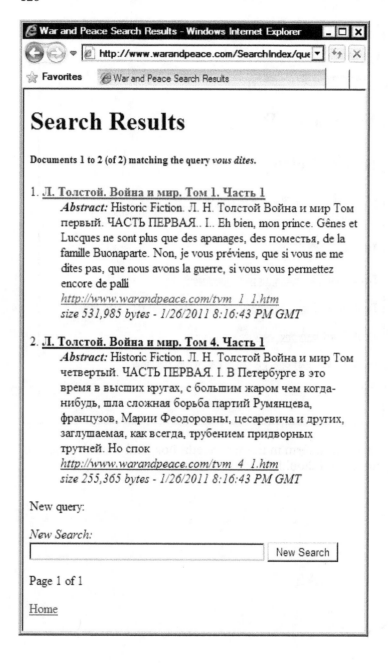

War and Peace Search Results - Windows Internet Explorer

http://www.warandpeace.com/SearchIndex/que

Favorites   War and Peace Search Results

Search Results

Documents 1 to 2 (of 2) matching the query *vous dites.*

1. Л. Толстой. Война и мир. Том 1. Часть 1
   Abstract: Historic Fiction. Л. Н. Толстой Война и мир Том
   первый. ЧАСТЬ ПЕРВАЯ.. I.. Eh bien, mon prince. Gênes et
   Lucques ne sont plus que des apanages, des поместья, de la
   famille Buonaparte. Non, je vous préviens, que si vous ne me
   dites pas, que nous avons la guerre, si vous vous permettez
   encore de palli
   http://www.warandpeace.com/tvm_1_1.htm
   size 531,985 bytes - 1/26/2011 8:16:43 PM GMT

2. Л. Толстой. Война и мир. Том 4. Часть 1
   Abstract: Historic Fiction. Л. Н. Толстой Война и мир Том
   четвертый. ЧАСТЬ ПЕРВАЯ. I. В Петербурге в это
   время в высших кругах, с большим жаром чем когда-
   нибудь, шла сложная борьба партий Румянцева,
   французов, Марии Феодоровны, цесаревича и других,
   заглушаемая, как всегда, трубением придворных
   трутней. Но спок
   http://www.warandpeace.com/tvm_4_1.htm
   size 255,365 bytes - 1/26/2011 8:16:43 PM GMT

New query:

New Search:

| | New Search |

Page 1 of 1

Home

In our example the design of the web site search is very simple. Modify the setup and template to suit the look and feel requirements of your web sites.

Microsoft Web Platform Installer

Windows Server 2008 R2 comes with many great features; many more are available as separate downloads. *Microsoft Web Platform Installer* is a tool that greatly simplifies downloading, installation, and keeping track of the add-ons to Windows Web Server.

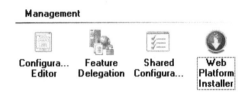

Web Platform Installer is available for download from the Microsoft web site. Once installed, launch Web Platform Installer from the Management section of the IIS Manager.

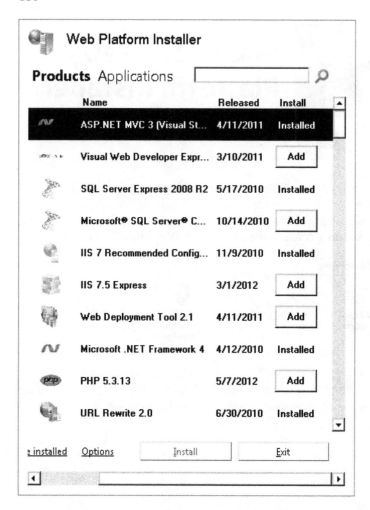

With Web Platform Installer you get access to many products and applications in different categories; and you can use the search box for quickly finding needed add-ons.

Let us review a couple of products available through Web Platform Installer.

Windows Media Services

Windows Server platform has provided functionality to stream audio and video for many versions. The current *Windows Media Services 2008 R2* is a member of the product line that started as *NetShow Server* in Windows NT of the 1990's.

Windows Media Services 2008 R2 allows delivering streaming media content in the following formats:

· Advanced Systems Format files (.asf).

· Windows Media Audio files (.wma).

· Windows Media Video files (.wmv).

· MP3 files (.mp3). Except multiple bit rate (MBR) encoded files.

· JPEG files (.jpeg or .jpg) for interstitial advertisements in playlists.

· Multicast information files (.nsc).

· Server-side playlist files (.wsx).

ASP.NET MVC

Windows Web Server 2008 R2 provides ability to serve web applications and services built on the extremely powerful and robust ASP.NET platform. Something that had been missing from the early versions of ASP.NET is the ability to create simple interactive web pages using as few as a single file, mixing HTML design and programming code together.

PHP, the ASP.NET competitor, has long provided the ability of creating simple dynamic web pages with nothing more than a simple text editor. The ASP.NET *Razor* engine now allows ASP.NET developers to do the same. If you need to quickly setup a dynamic form on your Windows Web Server 2008 R2 hosted web site, you can do it in a *.cshtml* (for C# code) or *.vbhtml* (for Visual Basic code) text file.

To enable serving *.cshtml* and *.vbhtml* files from IIS on your Windows Web Server, install the latest version of *ASP.NET MVC* product.

12 Before Going Live

Basic Security Checks

First and foremost, be advised that securing your server is outside of the scope of this book. Go ahead and get a tome or a few on the subject of Internet Security. Furthermore, Internet Security is a constantly changing filed. Hackers keep on coming up with new methods to break and exploit computer systems, while it is the job of server administrators to fend off the attacks. We do nevertheless want to lightly touch on several selected topics.

As soon as you connect your server to the Internet, it will be bombarded by hackers trying to break in. Every Windows Server 2008 R2 installation comes with a built-in administrator user. By default that user's name is *Administrator*. A great deal of the attacks will assume you had not renamed the default administrator account. Rename it. Also, change the workgroup name from the default *WORKGROUP* to something else.

You probably heard a million times that good password policy is important. Change passwords often, and pick good passwords. A password such as "p@$$word" is terrible and will be broken in seconds. A password similar to "HY4S$p3g#daX" is a much better password.

Investigate the need to put an antivirus on your server. Microsoft Forefront/System Center Endpoint Protection client is one such solution to seek out malware and rootkits.

Keep your computer up to date. Download and run the latest version of the Microsoft Baseline Security Analyzer (MBSA) to scan for common security misconfigurations.

A type of attack you hear a lot about in the media is the *Distributed Denial of Service (DDoS) Attack*. You will not be able to protect your server from a serious DDoS attack just from within the operating system. Discuss with your Internet services provider how such attacks will be mitigated and what levels of protection are available.

Not all Internet services providers offer DDoS protection in-house; if you need DDoS protection then chose a provider who does, or try the so called DDoS protection *Proxy*. With the latter, you receive a dedicated IP address and then you point your DNS A records to that address so that all incoming IP packets go through the Proxy before they are routed to your server.

The DDoS protection Proxy constantly monitors traffic, and once it senses an attack it filters out malicious packets. Keep in mind that DDoS protection services can be conveniently combined with load balancing. Once your DDoS protection is up and running make sure to test if there is any negative impact on your server access performance and response times.

Good DDoS protection is expensive. If your services are not likely to become a target of DDoS attacks, a possible strategy is to plan for your server becoming unreachable as your Internet services provider null-routes (sends to nowhere) the traffic to your server for the duration of an attack.

Even when you are not the target of a DDoS attack, if your server is not properly secured hackers may utilize it as an amplifier for a distributed reflected denial of service (DRDoS) attack on somebody else.

For example, never send a larger UDP packet to answer a small UDP packet from a non-authenticated source. If this is allowed to happen, a hacker, using very little of his bandwidth, can send small packets with a spoofed IP address, making your server send larger packets over your bandwidth to the IP address being attacked.

Intrusion Detection and Prevention

While your server needs outside help to deal with DDoS assaults, there is a great deal of attacks it is perfectly capable of fending on its own.

For example, when a web request hits Internet Information Services, the request is validated by a special helper. If the helper notices something malicious, such as a request URL that is too large, the request would be dropped, and an entry made in the event log, including the corresponding data and the address from which the request came from.

As you can imagine a lot of security measures are already built into the Windows Server operating system. Where before, some components such as *UrlScan* (a filter that restricts the types of HTTP requests that Internet Information Services web server will process) and *Best Practices Analyzer* had to be obtained separately, with Windows Server 2008 R2 they are employed by default or are only a few clicks away.

Windows Server versions went from having no built-in firewall at all, to a basic firewall, and to the current Windows Firewall with Advanced Security we discussed a few chapters earlier.

Microsoft constantly releases updates to the Windows Server to patch discovered vulnerabilities and to prevent new types of attacks. Keeping your installation of Windows Server 2008 R2 patched with all the updates installed is very important.

Additional security comes from employing an Intrusion Detection System (IDS). Such system can be located on the network – network based – or run on the server itself – host based. The IDS must have access to the IP traffic on the server's Internet interface.

At the rudimentary functionality level the IDS analyzes IP packets by comparing them to known malicious signatures and deviations from standard protocols. The IDS may also perform such advanced forms of network traffic analysis as statistical anomaly detection.

Passive IDS would register an attack and possibly notify the administrator. More useful for a live web server is reactive IDS, also known as intrusion prevention system (IPS) or intrusion detection and prevention system (IDPS). Once the attack is detected, reactive IDS would move to mitigate it. If this is an in-line system it can work by dropping malicious packets; otherwise it may automatically reprogram firewall to block the invader.

13 Switching IPs between Testing and Live Connections

In the *"IP Addresses for Pre-Deployment"* chapter we demonstrated how to use the Microsoft Loopback Adapter for binding to IP addresses before the server is actually connected to the Internet. In this chapter we will discuss how to easily switch back and forth between the *testing* loopback connection and the *live* network connection on the physical network adapter.

Our goal is to create a pair of batch files. Executing one would put the server in the stand-alone testing mode, where all IP addresses are assigned to the loopback adapter. Executing the other batch file would assign the IP addresses to the live network adapter.

First, let us review the configuration. Again our configuration is for demonstration purposes; substitute the IP addresses and network adapter names with what you have configured for your actual server usage.

We are using the following IP addresses.

    172.31.133.10
    172.31.133.11
    172.31.133.12
    172.31.133.13
    172.31.133.14

Our subnet mask is: 255.255.255.248

Our gateway address is: 172.31.133.9

Our loopback adapter connection name is *Local Loopback Connection*" and our live network adapter connection name is *"Live Datacenter Connection."* By default Windows Server 2008 R2 names local network connections: "Local Area Connection," "Local Area Connection 1," "Local Area Connection 2," and so on.

We recommend that you change your connection names to more meaningful identifiers; this can be easily done from the Network Connections control panel applet (ncpa.cpl). Simply right click on a connection you want to rename, and choose "Rename" from the pop-up menu.

To do the grunt work on changing the IP configuration we will use the *netsh* utility in script mode. We will write two scripts, one for switching to loopback mode, and another for switching to live mode; and our two batch files will simply call the netsh utility with one or the other script.

Create a folder for your script and batch files. Our examples assume your batch and script files are located in the same folder, from which the batch files execute.

Before we venture further, it is worth noting that you can use the following netsh command to dump your IPv4 configuration to a text file (*nssscript_ipv4_config.txt* in this case). You may find it useful to start from such a file, instead of writing netsh scripts from scratch.

```
netsh -c interface ipv4 dump > nssscript_ipv4_config.txt
```

Now let us go ahead and create the first script file named *nsscript_switch_to_loopback.txt* with the following content.

```
# ---------------------------------
# IPv4 Configuration
# ---------------------------------
pushd interface ipv4

delete address name="Live Datacenter Connection" address=172.31.133.14
delete address name="Live Datacenter Connection" address=172.31.133.13
delete address name="Live Datacenter Connection" address=172.31.133.12
delete address name="Live Datacenter Connection" address=172.31.133.11
delete address name="Live Datacenter Connection" address=172.31.133.10
```

```
delete route prefix=0.0.0.0/0 interface="Live Datacenter Connection"
nexthop=172.31.133.9

set global icmpredirects=enabled

add route prefix=0.0.0.0/0 interface="Local Loopback Connection" nexthop=172.31.133.9
publish=Yes
add address name="Local Loopback Connection" address=172.31.133.10
mask=255.255.255.248
add address name="Local Loopback Connection" address=172.31.133.11
mask=255.255.255.248 skipassource=true
add address name="Local Loopback Connection" address=172.31.133.12
mask=255.255.255.248 skipassource=true
add address name="Local Loopback Connection" address=172.31.133.13
mask=255.255.255.248 skipassource=true
add address name="Local Loopback Connection" address=172.31.133.14
mask=255.255.255.248 skipassource=true


popd
# End of IPv4 configuration
```

As you can see, this script file instructs removal of IP addresses from one adapter, and then addition of the same IP addresses to the other.

Now create a batch file. Name this file "*Switch IPs to Loopback. bat*." The content of this file follows.

```
echo Switching IPs to the Loopback Connection
netsh -f nsscript_switch_to_loopback.txt
pause
```

The batch file calls the netsh utility and tells it to execute the nss-cript_switch_to_loopback.txt script. The *pause* command keeps the batch execute window open until a key is pressed, so you can see if any errors pop up.

By simply switching what connection the IPs get deleted from and assigned to, create another pair of files.

nsscript_switch_to_live.txt:

```
# ---------------------------------
# IPv4 Configuration
# ---------------------------------
pushd interface ipv4

delete address name="Local Loopback Connection" address=172.31.133.14
delete address name="Local Loopback Connection" address=172.31.133.13
delete address name="Local Loopback Connection" address=172.31.133.12
delete address name="Local Loopback Connection" address=172.31.133.11
delete address name="Local Loopback Connection" address=172.31.133.10
delete route prefix=0.0.0.0/0 interface="Local Loopback Connection"
nexthop=172.31.133.9

set global icmpredirects=enabled

add route prefix=0.0.0.0/0 interface="Live Datacenter Connection" nexthop=172.31.133.9
publish=Yes
add address name="Live Datacenter Connection" address=172.31.133.10
mask=255.255.255.248
add address name="Live Datacenter Connection" address=172.31.133.11
mask=255.255.255.248 skipassource=true
add address name="Live Datacenter Connection" address=172.31.133.12
mask=255.255.255.248 skipassource=true
add address name="Live Datacenter Connection" address=172.31.133.13
mask=255.255.255.248 skipassource=true
add address name="Live Datacenter Connection" address=172.31.133.14
mask=255.255.255.248 skipassource=true


popd
# End of IPv4 configuration
```

Switch IPs to Live.bat:

```
echo Switching IPs to the Live Datacenter Connection
netsh -f nsscript_switch_to_live.txt
pause
```

Now simply by double clicking on the *Switch IPs to Loopback.bat* file, you activate testing mode where IPs are bound to the loopback connection. And by double clicking on *Switch IPs to Live. bat* you activate the live Internet connection.

One thing to note is that our scripts do not touch the DNS Server settings; as such you would typically configure the live datacenter connection with DNS addresses your ISP gave you, and for the loopback DNS settings you would use IP addresses of your DNS server if you have one configured.

Last but not least, we made switching IP configuration so easy that you may accidently lock yourself out of the server and the server out of the Internet just by double clicking on the *Switch IPs to Loopback.bat* while accessing the server remotely through in-band management. So, once your server is ready for deployment and you are done with all the tests, change the extension of the batch files to something that does not gets executed automatically when double-clicked.

14 Enabling Remote Desktop

As we discussed in the "Remote Server Management" subsection of the "Selecting Hardware" section of the "Before you begin" chapter, early in the book, *Remote Desktop* is a convenient way of managing the server while being away from it. To enable remote desktop follow the steps in this chapter.

Launch the System Properties control panel applet (sysdm.cpl). And activate the "Remote" tab.

Under "Remote Desktop" select the following option: "Allow connections only from computers running Remote Desktop with Network Level Authentication (more secure)."

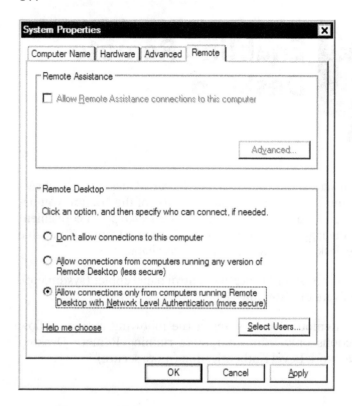

You will see the following warning:

"Remote Desktop Firewall exception will be enabled

You chose to enable Remote Desktop Connection for all network connections on this computer.

To enable it for selected network connections, open Windows Firewall with Advanced Security."

Click the OK button to accept. Then click OK to save the System Properties and exit the System Properties control panel applet.

Enabling Remote Desktop creates a security risk. As soon as your server is connected to the Internet Remote Desktop connections will be one of the ways hackers will try to get through. Following are a few ideas on making Remote Desktop more secure.

Make sure you use strong passwords. It is also a good idea to change the built-in administrator account name from "Administrator" to something else.

Access to remote desktop is controlled by the two following inbound rules in the Windows Firewall with Advanced Security.

- Remote Desktop (TCP-In)
- Remote Desktop - RemoteFX (TCP-In)

If you have a benefit of accessing your server remotely from locations with fixed public IP addresses, you can alter the scope of the firewall rules to allow connection from only your particular remote IP addresses.

By default, Remote Desktop listens on the TCP/IP port number 3389. To make it harder for hackers to spot that you have Remote Desktop enabled (although more determined hackers will use port scanners to find all ports you have open) you can change this port number to some other unused port number. Here is how.

First, create new firewall rules that mimic the two built-in firewall rules for the remote desktop. The new rules will differ from the built-in rules by the port number; they should open the port number you decided to use for Remote Desktop.

Second, find the *PortNumber* value and change it to your new chosen port number in the following registry key.

[HKEY_LOCAL_MACHINE\SYSTEM\CurrentControlSet\Control\
Terminal Server\WinStations\RDP-Tcp]

Then, restart your server for the change to take place.

You will now have to specify the port number (following a colon after the server name or address) when accessing your server from a Remote Desktop Client.

Remote Desktop in Windows Server 2008 R2 supports Transport Layer Security (TLS). Consider configuring a certificate and requiring SSL for remote desktop sessions. These settings are available by right-clicking on the RDP-Tcp connection in the Remote Desktop Session Host Configuration (tsconfig.msc) management console snap-in and selecting "Properties" from the pop-up menu.

In conclusion, once again we want to mention that it is very important that you have your server patched up with all the latest security updates.

Appendix I: Run Shortcuts

Control Panel Applets

Administrators use Control Panel to view and change Windows system settings. There is a variety of control panel applets to control various aspects of the system: hardware, software, region settings, and many more. Third party vendors may also install control panel applets on your system. To get to a needed applet quickly, you can type the applet name and extension in the Start button command bar and hit Enter.

appwiz.cpl – Control Panel\Programs\Programs and Features

desk.cpl – Control Panel\Appearance and Personalization\Display\Screen Resolution

Firewall.cpl – Control Panel\All Control Panel Items\Windows Firewall

hdwwiz.cpl – Device Manager

inetcpl.cpl – Internet Explorer Properties

intl.cpl – Region and Language settings

main.cpl – Mouse Properties

mmsys.cpl – Windows Audio Service settings

ncpa.cpl – Control Panel\All Control Panel Items\Network Connections

powercfg.cpl – Control Panel\All Control Panel Items\Power Options

sysdm.cpl – System Properties

telephon.cpl – Phone Modem settings

timedate.cpl – Date and Time

Management Console Snap-ins

Following is a list of Microsoft Management Console (MMC) snap-ins common on Windows 2008 R2 Web Server installations. MMC snap-ins are interactive tools used to manage various services and perform administrative tasks. Your list may differ, depending on what components are installed on your server. Just like the control panel wizards, MMC snap-ins can be called directly from the "Start – Run" line.

azman.msc – Authorization Manager

certmgr.msc – Certificate Manager

CIADV.MSC – Indexing Service Manager

comexp.msc – Component Services

compmgmt.msc – Computer Management

devmgmt.msc – Device Manager

diskmgmt.msc – Disk Management

dnsmgmt.msc – DNS Manager

eventvwr.msc – Event Viewer

fsmgmt.msc – Shared Folders Manager

fsrm.msc – File Server Resource Manager

gpedit.msc – Local Group Policy Editor

lusrmgr.msc – Local Users and Groups Manager

NAPCLCFG.MSC – Network Access Protection (NAP) Client Configuration

perfmon.msc – Performance Monitor

rsop.msc – Resultant Set of Policy Viewer

secpol.msc – Local Security Policy Editor

ServerManager.msc – Server manager

services.msc – Services Manager

SQLServerManager10.msc – SQL Server Configuration Manager

StorageMgmt.msc – Share and Storage Management

StorExpl.msc – Storage Explorer

tapimgmt.msc – Telephony Manager

taskschd.msc – Task Scheduler

tpm.msc – Trusted Platform Module (TPM) Manager

tsadmin.msc – Remote Desktop Services Manager

tsconfig.msc – Remote Desktop Session Host Configuration

tsmmc.msc – Remote Desktops Manager

wbadmin.msc – Windows Server Backup Manager

WF.msc – Windows Firewall with Advanced Security

WmiMgmt.msc – Windows Management Instrumentation (WMI) Console

Directory Shortcuts

Windows operating system comes with a rich directory structure. Among others; there is a directory where operating system files are located, directories for user data, and directories for applications.

Directory shortcuts serve two purposes. First, this is an easy way to figure out where something is located or supposed to be placed in.

Second, directory shortcuts can be used to quickly get to the needed folders from the Start menu Run bar, or from the Widows Explorer address bar.

Variable	Location
%ALLUSERSPROFILE%	Program data, default = %SYSTEMDRIVE%\ProgramData
%APPDATA%	%SYSTEMDRIVE%\Users\{username}\AppData\Roaming
%COMMONPROGRAM-FILES%	%SYSTEMDRIVE%\Common Files
%COMMONPROGRAM-FILES(x86)%	%SYSTEMDRIVE%\Program Files (x86)\Common Files
%HOMEDRIVE%	The user's home directory drive, default = C:
%HOMEPATH%	%SYSTEMDRIVE%\Users\{username}
%LOCALAPPDATA%	%SYSTEMDRIVE%\Users\{username}\AppData\Local
%PROGRAMDATA%	Program data, default = %SYSTEMDRIVE%\ProgramData
%PROGRAMFILES%	%SYSTEMDRIVE%\Program Files

%PROGRAMFILES(X86)%	%SYSTEMDRIVE%\ Program Files (x86)
%PSMODULEPATH%	%SystemRoot%\system32\ WindowsPowerShell\v1.0\ Modules\
%PUBLIC%	%SYSTEMDRIVE%\Users\ Public
%SYSTEMDRIVE%	The drive or partition where Windows is installed, default = C:
%SYSTEMROOT%	%WINDIR%
%TEMP% and %TMP%	%SYSTEMDRIVE%\Users\ {username}\AppData\Local\ Temp (or a subdirectory)
%USERPROFILE%	%SYSTEMDRIVE%\Users\ {username}
%WINDIR%	Windows directory, default = %SYSTEMDRIVE%\ Windows

Redirection for 32-bit Processes

Windows maintains a special directory for common *dynamically linked library* (DLL) files and other special use. The shortcut to that directory is as follows.

%SYSTEMROOT%\System32\

Please note that when accessing *%SYSTEMROOT%\System32*, 32-bit processes are automatically redirected to the *SysWOW64* folder (as 32-bit processes expect 32-bit versions of the needed DLLs). There are a few of the *System32* subdirectories for which such redirection is disabled (in other words, the 32-bit processes will see the actual subdirectories under System32 folder, not under SysWOW64 folder; but only for these particular shortcuts). The following is the list of the subdirectories for which the redirection is disabled.

%SYSTEMROOT%\System32\catroot

%SYSTEMROOT%\System32\catroot2

%SYSTEMROOT%\System32\drivers\etc

%SYSTEMROOT%\System32\logfiles

%SYSTEMROOT%\System32\spool

Similarly to System32 redirection, when sensing the *%PROGRAMFILES%* shortcut, Windows automatically redirects requests from 32-bit processes to *%PROGRAMFILES(X86)%*.

Some redirection and reflection (sharing of data with 64-bit branches) for 32-bit processes also happens when accessing specific keys in Windows registry.

Appendix II: Common Port Numbers

Following is a list of well-known and some official and unofficial *Internet Protocol* (IP) socket port numbers we compiled from the open sources on the Internet. For most recent information, please consult corresponding lists published by *Internet Assigned Numbers Authority* (IANA) and other online resources.

Wikipedia, by Wikimedia Foundation, Inc., maintains a list of TCP and UDP port numbers. That list is constantly updated by the Wikipedia web site contributors and is a great resource when looking up what software is known to run on particular port numbers.

Various security firms maintain lists of port numbers often used by Trojans, key loggers, worms, and other malicious software.

Note that software may be configured to run on any port number. Just because you see communication on a numbered port, it does not guarantee that listed software is responsible.

Port #		UDP	Description
0	TCP	UDP	Reserved
1	TCP	UDP	TCP Port Service Multiplexer (TCPMUX)
2	TCP	UDP	CompressNET Management Utility
3	TCP	UDP	CompressNET Compression Process

4	TCP	UDP	Unassigned
5	TCP	UDP	Remote Job Entry
7	TCP	UDP	Echo Protocol
8	TCP	UDP	Unassigned
9	TCP	UDP	Discard Protocol
10	TCP	UDP	Unassigned
11	TCP	UDP	Active Users (systat service)
12	TCP	UDP	Unassigned
13	TCP	UDP	Daytime Protocol (RFC 867)
14	TCP	UDP	Unassigned
15	TCP	UDP	Netstat service
16	TCP	UDP	Unassigned
17	TCP	UDP	Quote of the Day
18	TCP	UDP	Message Send Protocol
19	TCP	UDP	Character Generator Protocol (CHARGEN)
20	TCP		FTP – data transfer
21	TCP		FTP – control (command)
22	TCP		Secure Shell (SSH) – secure logins, file transfers (scp, sftp) and port forwarding

23	TCP		Telnet protocol – text communications
24	TCP	UDP	Priv-mail: any private mail system.
25	TCP		Simple Mail Transfer Protocol (SMTP) – e-mail routing between mail servers
26	TCP	UDP	Unassigned
27	TCP	UDP	NSW User System FE
29	TCP	UDP	MSG ICP
33	TCP	UDP	Display Support Protocol
35	TCP	UDP	Any private printer server protocol
37	TCP	UDP	TIME protocol
39	TCP	UDP	Resource Location Protocol (RLP)
40	TCP	UDP	Unassigned
42	TCP	UDP	ARPA Host Name Server Protocol
42	TCP	UDP	Windows Internet Name Service
43	TCP		WHOIS protocol
47	TCP	UDP	NI FTP
49	TCP	UDP	TACACS Login Host protocol
50	TCP	UDP	Remote Mail Checking Protocol
51	TCP	UDP	IMP Logical Address Maintenance

52	TCP	UDP	XNS (Xerox Network Systems) Time Protocol
53	TCP	UDP	Domain Name System (DNS)
54	TCP	UDP	XNS (Xerox Network Systems) Clearinghouse
55	TCP	UDP	ISI Graphics Language (ISI-GL)
56	TCP	UDP	XNS (Xerox Network Systems) Authentication
56	TCP	UDP	Route Access Protocol (RAP)
57	TCP		Mail Transfer Protocol (RFC 780)
58	TCP	UDP	XNS (Xerox Network Systems) Mail
67		UDP	Bootstrap Protocol (BOOTP) server; Dynamic Host Configuration Protocol (DHCP) server
68		UDP	Bootstrap Protocol (BOOTP) client; Dynamic Host Configuration Protocol (DHCP) client
69		UDP	Trivial File Transfer Protocol (TFTP)
70	TCP		Gopher protocol
71	TCP		NETRJS protocol
72	TCP		NETRJS protocol
73	TCP		NETRJS protocol

74	TCP		NETRJS protocol
79	TCP		Finger protocol
80	TCP		Hypertext Transfer Protocol (HTTP)
81	TCP		Torpark – routing
82		UDP	Torpark – control
88	TCP	UDP	Kerberos – authentication system
90	TCP	UDP	dnsix (DoD Network Security for Information Exchange) Securit Attribute Token Map
90	TCP	UDP	Pointcast
99	TCP		WIP Message protocol
101	TCP		NIC host name
102	TCP		ISO-TSAP (Transport Service Access Point)
104	TCP	UDP	ACR/NEMA Digital Imaging and Communications in Medicine
105	TCP	UDP	CCSO Nameserver Protocol (Qi/Ph)
107	TCP		Remote TELNET Service protocol
108	TCP	UDP	SNA Gateway Access Server
109	TCP		Post Office Protocol v2 (POP2)

110	TCP		Post Office Protocol v3 (POP3)
111	TCP	UDP	ONC RPC (SunRPC)
113	TCP		Ident – Authentication Service/ Identification Protocol, used by IRC servers to identify users
113		UDP	Authentication Service (auth)
115	TCP		Simple File Transfer Protocol (SFTP)
117	TCP		UUCP Path Service
118	TCP	UDP	SQL (Structured Query Language) Services
119	TCP		Network News Transfer Protocol (NNTP) – retrieval of newsgroup messages
123		UDP	Network Time Protocol (NTP) – time synchronization
135	TCP	UDP	DCE endpoint resolution (End Point Mapper), Remote Procedure Call (RPC), Messenger Service
137	TCP	UDP	NetBIOS Name Service
138	TCP	UDP	NetBIOS Datagram Service
139	TCP	UDP	NetBIOS Session Service
143	TCP		Internet Message Access Protocol (IMAP) – management of email messages

152	TCP	UDP	Background File Transfer Program (BFTP)
153	TCP	UDP	SGMP, Simple Gateway Monitoring Protocol
156	TCP	UDP	SQL Service
158	TCP	UDP	DMSP, Distributed Mail Service Protocol
161		UDP	Simple Network Management Protocol (SNMP)
162	TCP	UDP	Simple Network Management Protocol Trap (SNMPTRAP)
170	TCP		Print-srv, Network PostScript
175	TCP		VMNET (IBM z/VM, z/OS & z/VSE - Network Job Entry(NJE))
177	TCP	UDP	X Display Manager Control Protocol (XDMCP)
179	TCP		BGP (Border Gateway Protocol)
194	TCP	UDP	Internet Relay Chat (IRC)
199	TCP	UDP	SMUX, SNMP Unix Multiplexer
201	TCP	UDP	AppleTalk Routing Maintenance
209	TCP	UDP	The Quick Mail Transfer Protocol
210	TCP	UDP	ANSI Z39.50

213	TCP	UDP	Internetwork Packet Exchange (IPX)
218	TCP	UDP	Message posting protocol (MPP)
220	TCP	UDP	Internet Message Access Protocol (IMAP), version 3
259	TCP	UDP	ESRO, Efficient Short Remote Operations
264	TCP	UDP	BGMP, Border Gateway Multicast Protocol
280	TCP	UDP	http-mgmt
308	TCP		Novastor Online Backup
311	TCP		Mac OS X Server Admin (AppleShare IP Web administration)
318	TCP	UDP	PKIX TSP, Time Stamp Protocol
319		UDP	Precision time protocol event messages
320		UDP	Precision time protocol general messages
350	TCP	UDP	MATIP – Type A, Mapping of Airline Traffic over Internet Protocol
351	TCP	UDP	MATIP – Type B, Mapping of Airline Traffic over Internet Protocol
366	TCP	UDP	ODMR, On-Demand Mail Relay
369	TCP	UDP	Rpc2portmap

370	TCP	UDP	codaauth2 – Coda authentication server
370		UDP	securecast1 – Outgoing packets to NAI servers
371	TCP	UDP	ClearCase albd
383	TCP	UDP	HP data alarm manager
384	TCP	UDP	A Remote Network Server System
387	TCP	UDP	AURP, AppleTalk Update-based Routing Protocol
389	TCP	UDP	Lightweight Directory Access Protocol (LDAP)
401	TCP	UDP	Uninterruptible Power Supply (UPS)
427	TCP	UDP	Service Location Protocol (SLP)
443	TCP		HTTPS (Hypertext Transfer Protocol over SSL/TLS)
444	TCP	UDP	SNPP, Simple Network Paging Protocol (RFC 1568)
445	TCP		Microsoft-DS Active Directory, Windows shares
445	TCP		Microsoft-DS SMB file sharing
464	TCP	UDP	Kerberos Change/Set password
465	TCP		URL Rendesvous Directory for SSM (Cisco protocol)

475	TCP	UDP	tcpnethaspsrv (Aladdin Knowledge Systems Hasp services)
497	TCP		Dantz Retrospect
500		UDP	Internet Security Association and Key Management Protocol (ISAKMP)
502	TCP	UDP	Modbus, Protocol
504	TCP	UDP	Citadel – multiservice protocol for dedicated clients of the Citadel groupware system
512	TCP		Rexec, Remote Process Execution
512		UDP	comsat, together with biff
513	TCP		rlogin
513		UDP	Who
514	TCP		Shell – used to execute non-interactive commands on a remote system (Remote Shell, rsh, remsh)
514		UDP	Syslog – used for system logging
515	TCP		Line Printer Daemon – print service
517		UDP	Talk
518		UDP	NTalk
520	TCP		efs, extended file name server
520		UDP	Routing Information Protocol (RIP)

524	TCP	UDP	NetWare Core Protocol (NCP), used for access to primary NetWare server, Time Synchronization, etc.
525		UDP	Timed, Timeserver
530	TCP	UDP	RPC
531	TCP	UDP	AOL Instant Messenger
532	TCP		netnews
533		UDP	netwall, Emergency Broadcasts
540	TCP		UUCP (Unix-to-Unix Copy Protocol)
542	TCP	UDP	commerce (Commerce Applications)
543	TCP		klogin, Kerberos login
544	TCP		kshell, Kerberos Remote shell
545	TCP		OSIsoft PI (VMS)
546	TCP	UDP	DHCPv6 client
547	TCP	UDP	DHCPv6 server
548	TCP		Apple Filing Protocol (AFP) over TCP
550	TCP	UDP	new-rwho, new-who
554	TCP	UDP	Real Time Streaming Protocol (RTSP)

556	TCP		Remotefs, RFS, rfs_server
560		UDP	rmonitor, Remote Monitor
561		UDP	monitor
563	TCP	UDP	NNTP protocol over TLS/SSL (NNTPS)
587	TCP		e-mail message submission (SMTP)
591	TCP		FileMaker 6.0 (and later) Web Sharing
593	TCP	UDP	HTTP RPC Ep Map, Remote procedure call over Hypertext Transfer Protocol, often used by Distributed Component Object Model services and Microsoft Exchange Server
604	TCP		TUNNEL profile, a protocol for BEEP peers to form an application layer tunnel
623		UDP	ASF Remote Management and Control Protocol (ASF-RMCP)
631	TCP	UDP	Internet Printing Protocol (IPP)
631	TCP	UDP	Common Unix Printing System (CUPS)
635	TCP	UDP	RLZ DBase
636	TCP	UDP	Lightweight Directory Access Protocol over TLS/SSL (LDAPS)

639	TCP	UDP	MSDP, Multicast Source Discovery Protocol
641	TCP	UDP	SupportSoft Nexus Remote Command (control/listening): A proxy gateway connecting remote control traffic
646	TCP	UDP	LDP, Label Distribution Protocol, a routing protocol used in MPLS networks
647	TCP		DHCP Failover protocol
648	TCP		RRP (Registry Registrar Protocol)
651	TCP	UDP	IEEE-MMS
653	TCP	UDP	SupportSoft Nexus Remote Command (data): A proxy gateway connecting remote control traffic
654	TCP		Media Management System (MMS) Media Management Protocol (MMP)
657	TCP	UDP	IBM RMC (Remote monitoring and Control) protocol, used by System p5 AIX Integrated Virtualization Manager (IVM) and Hardware Management Console to connect managed logical partitions (LPAR) to enable dynamic partition reconfiguration
660	TCP		Mac OS X Server administration
666		UDP	Doom, first online first-person shooter

674	TCP		ACAP (Application Configuration Access Protocol)
691	TCP		MS Exchange Routing
694	TCP	UDP	Linux-HA High availability Heartbeat
695	TCP		IEEE-MMS-SSL (IEEE Media Management System over SSL)
698		UDP	OLSR (Optimized Link State Routing)
700	TCP		EPP (Extensible Provisioning Protocol), a protocol for communication between domain name registries and registrars (RFC 5734)
701	TCP		LMP (Link Management Protocol) – traffic engineering (TE) links management
702	TCP		IRIS (Internet Registry Information Service) over BEEP (Blocks Extensible Exchange Protocol) (RFC 3983)
706	TCP		Secure Internet Live Conferencing (SILC)
711	TCP		Cisco Tag Distribution Protocol – replaced by the MPLS Label Distribution Protocol
712	TCP		Topology Broadcast based on Reverse-Path Forwarding routing protocol (TBRPF) (RFC 3684)

749	TCP	UDP	Kerberos (protocol) administration
750		UDP	kerberos-iv, Kerberos version IV
751	TCP	UDP	kerberos_master, Kerberos authentication
752		UDP	passwd_server, Kerberos Password (kpasswd) server
753	TCP	UDP	Reverse Routing Header (rrh)
753		UDP	userreg_server, Kerberos userreg server
754	TCP		tell send
754	TCP		krb5_prop, Kerberos v5 slave propagation
754		UDP	tell send
760	TCP	UDP	krbupdate , Kerberos registration
782	TCP		Conserver serial – console management server
783	TCP		SpamAssassin spamd daemon
808	TCP		Microsoft Net.TCP Port Sharing Service
829	TCP		Certificate Management Protocol
843	TCP		Adobe Flash
847	TCP		DHCP Failover protocol

848	TCP	UDP	Group Domain Of Interpretation (GDOI) protocol
860	TCP		iSCSI (RFC 3720)
873	TCP		rsync file synchronisation protocol
888	TCP		cddbp, CD DataBase (CDDB) protocol (CDDBP)
901	TCP		Samba Web Administration Tool (SWAT)
901	TCP	UDP	VMware Virtual Infrastructure Client
902	TCP		ideafarm-door
902	TCP	UDP	VMware Server Console
902		UDP	ideafarm-door
903	TCP		VMware Remote Console
904	TCP		VMware Server Alternate (if 902 is in use)
911	TCP		Network Console on Acid (NCA) – local TTY redirection over OpenSSH
944		UDP	Network File System (protocol) Service
953	TCP	UDP	Domain Name System (DNS) RNDC Service

973		UDP	Network File System (protocol) over IPv6 Service
981	TCP		SofaWare Technologies Remote HTTPS management for firewalls
989	TCP	UDP	FTPS Protocol (data): FTP over TLS/SSL
990	TCP	UDP	FTPS Protocol (control): FTP over TLS/SSL
991	TCP	UDP	NAS (Netnews Administration System)
992	TCP	UDP	TELNET protocol over TLS/SSL
993	TCP		Internet Message Access Protocol over SSL (IMAPS)
995	TCP		Post Office Protocol 3 over TLS/SSL (POP3S)
999	TCP		ScimoreDB Database System
1002	TCP		Opsware agent (aka cogbot)
1023	TCP	UDP	Reserved
1024	TCP	UDP	Reserved
1025	TCP		NFS or IIS or Teradata
1026	TCP		Often used by Microsoft DCOM services
1029	TCP		Often used by Microsoft DCOM services

1058	TCP	UDP	nim, IBM AIX Network Installation Manager (NIM)
1059	TCP	UDP	nimreg, IBM AIX Network Installation Manager (NIM)
1080	TCP		SOCKS proxy
1085	TCP	UDP	WebObjects
1098	TCP	UDP	rmiactivation, RMI Activation
1099	TCP	UDP	rmiregistry, RMI Registry
1109	TCP		Kerberos Post Office Protocol (KPOP)
1110		UDP	EasyBits School network discovery protocol (for Intel's CMPC platform)
1140	TCP	UDP	AutoNOC protocol
1167		UDP	phone, conference calling
1169	TCP	UDP	Tripwire
1176	TCP		Perceptive Automation Indigo Home automation server
1182	TCP	UDP	AcceleNet Intelligent Transfer Protocol
1194	TCP	UDP	OpenVPN
1198	TCP	UDP	The cajo project dynamic transparent distributed computing in Java

1200	TCP	UDP	scol, SCOL 3D virtual worlds name resolution
1200		UDP	Steam Friends Applet
1214	TCP		Kazaa
1217	TCP		Uvora Online
1220	TCP		QuickTime Streaming Server administration
1223	TCP	UDP	TGP, TrulyGlobal Protocol, also known as "The Gur Protocol" (named for Gur Kimchi of TrulyGlobal)
1234		UDP	VLC media player default port for UDP/RTP stream
1236	TCP		Symantec BindView Control UNIX Default port for TCP management server connections
1241	TCP	UDP	Nessus Security Scanner
1270	TCP	UDP	Microsoft System Center Operations Manager (SCOM) agent
1293	TCP	UDP	IPSec (Internet Protocol Security)
1301	TCP		Palmer Performance OBDNet
1309	TCP		Altera Quartus jtagd
1311	TCP		Dell OpenManage HTTPS
1319	TCP		AMX ICSP

1319		UDP	AMX ICSP
1337	TCP	UDP	Men and Mice DNS
1337	TCP		PowerFolder P2P Encrypted File Synchronization Program
1337	TCP		WASTE Encrypted File Sharing Program
1344	TCP		Internet Content Adaptation Protocol
1352	TCP		IBM Lotus Notes/Domino (RPC) protocol
1387	TCP	UDP	cadsi-lm, LMS International (formerly Computer Aided Design Software, Inc. (CADSI)) LM
1414	TCP		IBM WebSphere MQ (formerly known as MQSeries)
1417	TCP	UDP	Timbuktu Service 1 Port
1418	TCP	UDP	Timbuktu Service 2 Port
1419	TCP	UDP	Timbuktu Service 3 Port
1420	TCP	UDP	Timbuktu Service 4 Port
1431	TCP		Reverse Gossip Transport Protocol (RGTP)
1433	TCP		MSSQL (Microsoft SQL Server database management system) Server

1434	TCP	UDP	MSSQL (Microsoft SQL Server database management system) Monitor
1470	TCP		Solarwinds Kiwi Log Server
1494	TCP		Citrix XenApp Independent Computing Architecture (ICA) thin client protocol
1500	TCP		NetGuard GuardianPro firewall (NT4-based) Remote Management
1501		UDP	NetGuard GuardianPro firewall (NT4-based) Authentication Client
1503	TCP	UDP	Windows Live Messenger (Whiteboard and Application Sharing)
1512	TCP	UDP	Microsoft Windows Internet Name Service (WINS)
1513	TCP	UDP	Garena Garena Gaming Client
1521	TCP		nCube License Manager
1521	TCP		Oracle database default listener, also see port 2483
1524	TCP	UDP	ingreslock, ingres
1526	TCP		Oracle database common alternative for listener
1527	TCP		Apache Derby Network Server default port

1533	TCP		IBM Sametime IM – Virtual Places Chat Microsoft SQL Server
1534		UDP	Eclipse Target Communication Framework (TCF) agent discovery
1547	TCP	UDP	Laplink
1550	TCP	UDP	3m-image-lm Image Storage license manager 3M Company
1581		UDP	MIL STD 2045-47001 VMF
1589		UDP	Cisco VQP (VLAN Query Protocol) / VMPS
1645	TCP	UDP	radius auth, RADIUS authentication protocol (default for Cisco and Juniper Networks RADIUS servers, also see port 1812)
1646	TCP	UDP	radius acct, RADIUS authentication protocol (default for Cisco and Juniper Networks RADIUS servers, also see port 1813)
1666	TCP		Perforce
1677	TCP	UDP	Novell GroupWise clients in client/ server access mode
1688	TCP		Microsoft Key Management Service for KMS Windows Activation
1701		UDP	Layer 2 Forwarding Protocol (L2F) & Layer 2 Tunneling Protocol (L2TP)

1707	TCP	UDP	Windward Studios
1707		TCP	Romtoc Packet Protocol (L2F) & Layer 2 Tunneling Protocol (L2TP)
1716	TCP		America's Army Massively multi-player online game (MMO)
1719		UDP	H.323 Registration and alternate communication
1720	TCP		H.323 Call signaling
1723	TCP	UDP	Microsoft Point-to-Point Tunneling Protocol (PPTP)
1725		UDP	Valve Steam Client
1755	TCP	UDP	Microsoft Media Services (MMS, ms-streaming)
1761	TCP	UDP	cft-0
1761	TCP		Novell Zenworks Remote Control utility
1762–1768	TCP	UDP	cft-1 to cft-7
1801	TCP	UDP	Microsoft Message Queuing
1812	TCP	UDP	radius, RADIUS authentication protocol
1813	TCP	UDP	radacct, RADIUS accounting protocol

1863	TCP		MSNP (Microsoft Notification Protocol), used by the .NET Messenger Service and a number of Instant Messaging clients
1883	TCP	UDP	MQ Telemetry Transport (MQTT), formerly known as MQIsdp (MQSeries SCADA protocol)
1886	TCP		Leonardo over IP Pro2col Ltd
1900		UDP	Microsoft SSDP Enables discovery of UPnP devices
1920	TCP		IBM Tivoli monitoring console
1935	TCP		Adobe Systems Macromedia Flash Real Time Messaging Protocol (RTMP)
1947	TCP	UDP	SentinelSRM (hasplm), Aladdin HASP License Manager
1970	TCP	UDP	Netop Business Solutions Netop Remote Control
1971	TCP	UDP	Netop Business Solutions Netop School
1972	TCP	UDP	InterSystems Caché
1975– 1977		UDP	Cisco TCO (Documentation)
1984	TCP		Big Brother and related Xymon (formerly Hobbit) System and Network Monitor

1985		UDP	Cisco HSRP
1994	TCP	UDP	Cisco STUN-SDLC (Serial Tunneling–Synchronous Data Link Control) protocol
1998	TCP	UDP	Cisco X.25 over TCP (XOT) service
2000	TCP	UDP	Cisco SCCP (Skinny)
2001		UDP	CAPTAN Test Stand System
2030			Oracle services for Microsoft Transaction Server
2031	TCP	UDP	mobrien-chat
2049		UDP	NFS (Network File System)
2049		UDP	Shilp
2053	TCP		knetd Kerberos de-multiplexor
2056		UDP	Civilization 4 multiplayer
2074	TCP	UDP	Vertel VMF SA (i.e. App.. SpeakFreely)
2080	TCP	UDP	Autodesk NLM (FLEXlm)
2082	TCP		Infowave Mobility Server
2082	TCP		CPanel default
2083	TCP		Secure Radius Service (radsec)
2083	TCP		CPanel default SSL

2086	TCP		GNUnet
2086	TCP		WebHost Manager default
2087	TCP		WebHost Manager default SSL
2095	TCP		CPanel default Web mail
2096	TCP		CPanel default SSL Web mail
2102	TCP	UDP	zephyr-srv Project Athena Zephyr Notification Service server
2103	TCP	UDP	zephyr-clt Project Athena Zephyr Notification Service serv-hm connection
2104	TCP	UDP	zephyr-hm Project Athena Zephyr Notification Service hostmanager
2105	TCP	UDP	IBM MiniPay
2105	TCP	UDP	eklogin Kerberos encrypted remote login (rlogin)
2156		UDP	Talari Reliable Protocol
2160	TCP		APC Agent
2161	TCP		APC Agent
2181	TCP	UDP	EForward – document transport system
2200		UDP	Tuxanci game server
2210	TCP	UDP	NOAAPORT Broadcast Network

2210	TCP		MikroTik Remote management for "The Dude"
2211	TCP	UDP	EMWIN
2211	TCP		MikroTik Secure management for "The Dude"
2212	TCP	UDP	LeeCO POS Server Service
2212	TCP		Port-A-Pour Remote WinBatch
2219	TCP	UDP	NetIQ NCAP Protocol
2220	TCP	UDP	NetIQ End2End
2221	TCP		ESET Anti-virus updates
2222	TCP		DirectAdmin default & ESET Remote Administration
2261	TCP	UDP	CoMotion Master
2262	TCP	UDP	CoMotion Backup
2302		UDP	ArmA multiplayer (default for game)
2302		UDP	Halo: Combat Evolved multiplayer
2303		UDP	ArmA multiplayer (server reporting, default port for game +1)
2305		UDP	ArmA multiplayer (default for VoN, default port for game +3)
2323	TCP		Philips TVs based on jointSPACE

2369	TCP		Default for BMC Software Control-M/Server–Configuration Agent
2370	TCP		Default for BMC Software Control-M/Server–to allow the Control-M/Enterprise Manager to connect to the Control-M/Server
2379	TCP		KGS Go Server
2401	TCP		CVS version control system
2404	TCP		IEC 60870-5-104, used to send electric power telecontrol messages
2420		UDP	Westell Remote Access
2427		UDP	Cisco MGCP
2447	TCP	UDP	ovwdb–OpenView Network Node Manager (NNM) daemon
2483	TCP	UDP	Oracle database listening for unsecure client connections to the listener, replaces port 1521
2484	TCP	UDP	Oracle database listening for SSL client connections to the listener
2500	TCP		THEÒSMESSENGER listening for TheòsMessenger client connections
2501	TCP		TheosNet-Admin listening for TheòsMessenger client connections
2518	TCP	UDP	Willy
2535	TCP		MADCAP

2546	TCP	UDP	EVault data protection services
2593	TCP	UDP	RunUO – Ultima Online server
2599	TCP		SonicWALL anti-spam traffic between Remote Analyzer (RA) and Control Center (CC)
2610	TCP		Dark Ages (video game)
2612	TCP	UDP	QPasa from MQSoftware
2636	TCP		Solve Service
2638	TCP		Sybase Adaptive Server Anywhere (SQL Anywhere)
2641	TCP	UDP	HDL Server from CNRI
2642	TCP	UDP	Tragic
2698	TCP	UDP	Citel / MCK IVPIP
2700–2800	TCP		KnowShowGo P2P
2710	TCP		XBT Tracker
2710		UDP	XBT Tracker experimental UDP tracker extension
2735	TCP	UDP	NetIQ Monitor Console
2809	TCP		corbaloc:iiop URL, per the CORBA 3.0.3 specification
2809	TCP		IBM WebSphere Application Server (WAS) Bootstrap/rmi default

2809		UDP	corbaloc:iiop URL, per the CORBA 3.0.3 specification.
2868	TCP	UDP	Norman Proprietary Event Protocol NPEP
2944		UDP	Megaco text H.248
2945		UDP	Megaco binary (ASN.1) H.248
2947	TCP		gpsd GPS daemon
2948	TCP	UDP	WAP-push Multimedia Messaging Service (MMS)
2949	TCP	UDP	WAP-pushsecure Multimedia Messaging Service (MMS)
2967	TCP		Symantec AntiVirus Corporate Edition
3000	TCP		Cloud9 Integrated Development Environment server
3000		UDP	Distributed Interactive Simulation (DIS), modifiable default
3000	TCP		Ruby on Rails development default
3001	TCP		Opsware server (Satellite)
3030	TCP	UDP	NetPanzer
3050	TCP	UDP	gds_db (Interbase/Firebird)
3051	TCP	UDP	Galaxy Server (Gateway Ticketing Systems)

3052	TCP	UDP	APC PowerChute Network
3074	TCP	UDP	Xbox LIVE and/or Games for Windows
3101	TCP		BlackBerry Enterprise Server communication to cloud
3119	TCP		D2000 Entis/Actis Application server
3128	TCP		Web caches and the default for the Squid (software)
3162	TCP	UDP	SFLM (Standard Floating License Manager)
3225	TCP	UDP	FCIP (Fiber Channel over Internet Protocol)
3233	TCP	UDP	WhiskerControl research control protocol
3235	TCP	UDP	Galaxy Network Service (Gateway Ticketing Systems)
3260	TCP		iSCSI target
3268	TCP	UDP	msft-gc, Microsoft Global Catalog (LDAP service which contains data from Active Directory forests)
3269	TCP	UDP	msft-gc-ssl, Microsoft Global Catalog over SSL (similar to port 3268, LDAP over SSL)

3283	TCP		Apple Remote Desktop reporting (officially Net Assistant, referring to an earlier product)
3299	TCP		SAP-Router (routing application proxy for SAP R/3)
3305	TCP	UDP	odette-ftp, Odette File Transfer Protocol (OFTP)
3306	TCP	UDP	MySQL database system
3313	TCP		Verisys file integrity monitoring software
3333	TCP		Network Caller ID server
3333	TCP		CruiseControl.rb
3386	TCP	UDP	GTP 3GPP GSM/UMTS CDR logging protocol
3389	TCP	UDP	Microsoft Terminal Server (RDP), Windows Based Terminal (WBT)
3396	TCP	UDP	Novell NDPS Printer Agent
3412	TCP	UDP	xmlBlaster
3455	TCP	UDP	[RSVP] Reservation Protocol
3423	TCP		Xware xTrm Communication Protocol
3424	TCP		Xware xTrm Communication Protocol over SSL
3478	TCP	UDP	STUN, a protocol for NAT traversal

3478	TCP	UDP	TURN, a protocol for NAT traversal
3483		UDP	Slim Devices discovery protocol
3483	TCP		Slim Devices SlimProto protocol
3516	TCP	UDP	Smartcard Port
3527		UDP	Microsoft Message Queuing
3535	TCP		SMTP alternate
3544		UDP	Teredo tunneling
3605		UDP	ComCam IO Port
3606	TCP	UDP	Splitlock Server
3632	TCP		distributed compiler
3689	TCP		Digital Audio Access Protocol (DAAP) – Apple iTunes and AirPort Express
3690	TCP	UDP	Subversion (SVN) version control system
3702	TCP	UDP	Web Services Dynamic Discovery (WS-Discovery), used by various components of Windows Vista
3723	TCP	UDP	Used by many Battle.net Blizzard games (Diablo II, Warcraft II, Warcraft III, StarCraft)
3724	TCP		World of Warcraft Online gaming MMORPG

3724	TCP		Club Penguin Disney online game for kids
3724		UDP	World of Warcraft Online gaming MMORPG
3784	TCP	UDP	VoIP program used by Ventrilo
3785		UDP	VoIP program used by Ventrilo
3799		UDP	RADIUS change of authorization
3880	TCP	UDP	IGRS
3868	TCP		Diameter base protocol (RFC 3588)
3899	TCP		Remote Administrator
3900	TCP		udt_os, IBM UniData UDT OS
3945	TCP	UDP	EMCADS service, a Giritech product used by G/On
3978	TCP	UDP	OpenTTD game (masterserver and content service)
3979	TCP	UDP	OpenTTD game
3999	TCP	UDP	Norman distributed scanning service
4000	TCP	UDP	Diablo II game
4001	TCP		Microsoft Ants game
4018	TCP	UDP	protocol information and warnings
4045	TCP	UDP	Solaris lockd NFS lock daemon/manager

4069		UDP	Minger Email Address Verification Protocol
4089	TCP	UDP	OpenCORE Remote Control Service
4093	TCP	UDP	PxPlus Client server interface ProvideX
4096	TCP	UDP	Ascom Timeplex BRE (Bridge Relay Element)
4100	TCP		WatchGuard authentication applet default
4111	TCP		Xgrid
4116	TCP	UDP	Smartcard-TLS
4125	TCP		Microsoft Remote Web Workplace administration
4172	TCP	UDP	Teradici PCoIP
4201	TCP		TinyMUD and various derivatives
4226	TCP	UDP	Aleph One (game)
4321	TCP		Referral Whois (RWhois) Protocol
4486	TCP	UDP	Integrated Client Message Service (ICMS)
4500		UDP	IPSec NAT Traversal (RFC 3947)
4502-4534	TCP		Microsoft Silverlight connectable ports under non-elevated trust

4534		UDP	Armagetron Advanced default server port
4567	TCP		Sinatra default server port in development mode (HTTP)
4569		UDP	Inter-Asterisk eXchange (IAX2)
4610–4640	TCP		QualiSystems TestShell Suite Services
4662	TCP	UDP	OrbitNet Message Service
4662	TCP		Default for older versions of eMule
4664	TCP		Google Desktop Search
4672		UDP	Default for older versions of eMule
4711	TCP		eMule optional web interface
4728	TCP		Computer Associates Desktop and Server Management (DMP)/Port Multiplexer
4747	TCP		Apprentice
4750	TCP		BladeLogic Agent
4840	TCP	UDP	OPC UA TCP Protocol for OPC Unified Architecture from OPC Foundation
4843	TCP	UDP	OPC UA TCP Protocol over TLS/SSL for OPC Unified Architecture from OPC Foundation

4847	TCP	UDP	Web Fresh Communication, Quadrion Software & Odorless Entertainment
4894	TCP	UDP	LysKOM Protocol A
4899	TCP	UDP	Radmin remote administration tool
4949	TCP		Munin Resource Monitoring Tool
4950	TCP	UDP	Cylon Controls UC32 Communications Port
5000	TCP		commplex-main
5000	TCP		UPnP–Windows network device interoperability
5000	TCP		VTun–VPN Software
5000		UDP	FlightGear multiplayer
5000		UDP	VTun–VPN Software
5001	TCP		commplex-link
5001	TCP		Slingbox and Slingplayer
5001	TCP	UDP	Iperf (Tool for measuring TCP and UDP bandwidth performance)
5002	TCP		SOLICARD ARX
5003	TCP	UDP	FileMaker
5004	TCP	UDP	RTP (Real-time Transport Protocol) media data (RFC 3551, RFC 4571)

5005	TCP	UDP	RTP (Real-time Transport Protocol) control protocol (RFC 3551, RFC 4571)
5050	TCP		Yahoo! Messenger
5051	TCP		ita-agent Symantec Intruder Alert
5060	TCP	UDP	Session Initiation Protocol (SIP)
5061	TCP		Session Initiation Protocol (SIP) over TLS
5070	TCP		Binary Floor Control Protocol (BFCP), RFC 4582. Also used for Session Initiation Protocol (SIP) preferred port for PUBLISH on SIP Trunk to Cisco Unified Presence Server (CUPS)
5082	TCP	UDP	Qpur Communication Protocol
5083	TCP	UDP	Qpur File Protocol
5084	TCP	UDP	EPCglobal Low Level Reader Protocol (LLRP)
5085	TCP	UDP	EPCglobal Low Level Reader Protocol (LLRP) over TLS
5093		UDP	SafeNet, Inc Sentinel LM, Sentinel RMS, License Manager, Client-to-Server
5099	TCP	UDP	SafeNet, Inc Sentinel LM, Sentinel RMS, License Manager, Server-to-Server

5104	TCP		IBM Tivoli Framework NetCOOL/ Impact HTTP Service
5110	TCP		ProRat Server
5121	TCP		Neverwinter Nights
5150	TCP	UDP	ATMP Ascend Tunnel Management Protocol
5151	TCP		ESRI SDE Instance
5151		UDP	ESRI SDE Remote Start
5154	TCP	UDP	BZFlag
5190	TCP		ICQ and AOL Instant Messenger
5222	TCP		Extensible Messaging and Presence Protocol (XMPP) client connection
5223	TCP		Extensible Messaging and Presence Protocol (XMPP) client connection over SSL
5228	TCP		HP Virtual Room Service
5228	TCP		Google Play
5246		UDP	Control And Provisioning of Wireless Access Points (CAPWAP) CAPWAP control
5247		UDP	Control And Provisioning of Wireless Access Points (CAPWAP) CAPWAP data

5269	TCP		Extensible Messaging and Presence Protocol (XMPP) server connection
5280	TCP		Extensible Messaging and Presence Protocol (XMPP) XEP-0124: Bidirectional-streams Over Synchronous HTTP (BOSH)
5281	TCP		Undo License Manager
5281	TCP		Extensible Messaging and Presence Protocol (XMPP)
5298	TCP	UDP	Extensible Messaging and Presence Protocol (XMPP)
5349	TCP		STUN, a protocol for NAT traversal (UDP is reserved)
5349	TCP		TURN, a protocol for NAT traversal (UDP is reserved)
5351	TCP	UDP	NAT Port Mapping Protocol–client-requested configuration for inbound connections through network address translators
5353		UDP	Multicast DNS (mDNS)
5355	TCP	UDP	LLMNR–Link-Local Multicast Name Resolution, allows hosts to perform name resolution for hosts on the same local link (only provided by Windows Vista and Server 2008)
5357	TCP	UDP	Web Services for Devices (WSDAPI)

5358	TCP	UDP	WSDAPI Applications to Use a Secure Channel
5402	TCP	UDP	mftp, Stratacache OmniCast content delivery system MFTP file sharing protocol
5405	TCP	UDP	NetSupport Manager
5412	TCP	UDP	IBM Rational Synergy (Telelogic_ Synergy) (Continuus CM) Message Router
5421	TCP	UDP	NetSupport Manager
5432	TCP	UDP	PostgreSQL database system
5433	TCP		Bouwsoft file/webserver
5450	TCP		OSIsoft PI Server Client Access
5457	TCP		OSIsoft PI Asset Framework Client Access
5458	TCP		OSIsoft PI Notifications Client Access
5495	TCP		Applix TM1 Admin server
5498	TCP		Hotline tracker server connection
5499		UDP	Hotline tracker server discovery
5500	TCP		VNC remote desktop protocol – for incoming listening viewer, Hotline control connection
5501	TCP		Hotline file transfer connection

5517	TCP		Setiqueue Proxy server client for SETI@Home project
5555	TCP		Freeciv versions up to 2.0, Hewlett-Packard Data Protector, McAfee EndPoint Encryption Database Server, SAP, Default for Microsoft Dynamics CRM 4.0
5556	TCP	UDP	Freeciv
5631	TCP		pcANYWHEREdata, Symantec pcAnywhere (version 7.52 and later) data
5632		UDP	pcANYWHEREstat, Symantec pcAnywhere (version 7.52 and later) status
5656	TCP		IBM Lotus Sametime p2p file transfer
5666	TCP		NRPE (Nagios)
5667	TCP		NSCA (Nagios)
5678		UDP	Mikrotik RouterOS Neighbor Discovery Protocol (MNDP)
5741	TCP	UDP	IDA Discover Port 1
5742	TCP	UDP	IDA Discover Port 2
5800	TCP		VNC remote desktop protocol – for use over HTTP

5900	TCP	UDP	Virtual Network Computing (VNC) remote desktop protocol (used by Apple Remote Desktop and others)
5938	TCP	UDP	TeamViewer remote desktop protocol
5984	TCP	UDP	CouchDB database server
5999	TCP		CVSup file update tool
6000	TCP		X11
6001		UDP	X11
6005	TCP		Default for BMC Software Control-M/Server–Socket used for communication between Control-M processes–though often changed during installation
6005	TCP		Default for Camfrog chat & cam client
6050	TCP		Arcserve backup
6051	TCP		Arcserve backup
6086	TCP		PDTP–FTP like file server in a P2P network
6100	TCP		Vizrt System
6100	TCP		Ventrilo authentication
6110	TCP	UDP	softcm, HP Softbench CM

6111	TCP	UDP	spc, HP Softbench Sub-Process Control
6112	TCP	UDP	"dtspcd"–a network daemon that accepts requests from clients to execute commands and launch applications remotely
6112	TCP		Blizzard's Battle.net gaming service, ArenaNet gaming service, Relic gaming sercive
6112–6113	TCP		Club Penguin Disney online game for kids
6129	TCP		DameWare Remote Control
6257		UDP	WinMX (see also 6699)
6260	TCP	UDP	planet M.U.L.E.
6262	TCP		Sybase Advantage Database Server
6343		UDP	SFlow, sFlow traffic monitoring
6346	TCP	UDP	gnutella-svc, gnutella (FrostWire, Limewire, Shareaza, etc.)
6347	TCP	UDP	gnutella-rtr, Gnutella alternate
6350	TCP	UDP	App Discovery and Access Protocol
6389	TCP		EMC CLARiiON
6432	TCP		PgBouncer - A connection pooler for PostgreSQL
6444	TCP	UDP	Sun Grid Engine–Qmaster Service

6445	TCP	UDP	Sun Grid Engine–Execution Service
6502	TCP	UDP	Netop Business Solutions - NetOp Remote Control
6522	TCP		Gobby (and other libobby-based software)
6523	TCP		Gobby 0.5 (and other libinfinity-based software)
6543		UDP	Paradigm Research & Development Jetnet default
6566	TCP		SANE (Scanner Access Now Easy) – SANE network scanner daemon
6571			Windows Live FolderShare client
6600	TCP		Music Playing Daemon (MPD)
6619	TCP	UDP	odette-ftps, Odette File Transfer Protocol (OFTP) over TLS/SSL
6660– 6669	TCP		Internet Relay Chat (IRC)
6679	TCP	UDP	Osorno Automation Protocol (OSAUT)
6679	TCP		IRC SSL (Secure Internet Relay Chat)
6697	TCP		IRC SSL (Secure Internet Relay Chat)
6699	TCP		WinMX (see also 6257)

6789	TCP		Campbell Scientific Loggernet Software
6881–6887	TCP	UDP	BitTorrent, part of full range of ports used most often
6888	TCP	UDP	MUSE
6888–6900	TCP	UDP	BitTorrent, part of full range of ports used most often
6891–6900	TCP	UDP	Windows Live Messenger (File transfer)
6901	TCP	UDP	Windows Live Messenger (Voice)
6901–6968	TCP	UDP	BitTorrent, part of full range of ports used most often
6969	TCP	UDP	acmsoda
6969	TCP		BitTorrent tracker
6970–6999	TCP	UDP	BitTorrent, part of full range of ports used most often
7000	TCP		Default for Vuze's built in HTTPS Bittorrent Tracker
7000–7001	TCP		Avira Server Management Console
7001	TCP		Default for BEA WebLogic HTTP server
7002	TCP		Default for BEA WebLogic HTTPS server

7005	TCP		Default for BMC Software Control-M/Server and Control-M/Agent for Agent-to-Server
7006	TCP		Default for BMC Software Control-M/Server and Control-M/Agent for Server-to-Agent
7010	TCP		Default for Cisco AON AMC (AON Management Console)
7023		UDP	Bryan Wilcutt T2-NMCS Protocol for SatCom Modems
7025	TCP		Zimbra LMTP – local mail delivery
7047	TCP		Zimbra conversion server
7133	TCP		Enemy Territory: Quake Wars
7171	TCP		Tibia
7312		UDP	Sibelius License Server
7400	TCP	UDP	RTPS (Real Time Publish Subscribe) DDS Discovery
7401	TCP	UDP	RTPS (Real Time Publish Subscribe) DDS User-Traffic
7402	TCP	UDP	RTPS (Real Time Publish Subscribe) DDS Meta-Traffic
7473	TCP	UDP	Rise: The Vieneo Province
7547	TCP	UDP	CPE WAN Management Protocol Technical Report 069

7615	TCP		ISL Online communication protocol
7670	TCP		BrettspielWelt BSW Boardgame Portal
7707		UDP	Killing Floor
7708		UDP	Killing Floor
7717		UDP	Killing Floor
7777	TCP		iChat server file transfer proxy
7777	TCP		Terraria default server
7831	TCP		Default used by Smartlaunch Internet Cafe Administration software
7915	TCP		Default for YSFlight server
7935	TCP		Fixed port used for Adobe Flash Debug Player to communicate with a debugger (Flash IDE, Flex Builder or fdb).
7937-9936	TCP	UDP	EMC2 (Legato) Networker or Sun Solcitice Backup
8000	TCP	UDP	iRDMI (Intel Remote Desktop Management Interface)
8000-8001	TCP		Internet radio streams such as SHOUTcast
8008	TCP		HTTP Alternate

8008	TCP		IBM HTTP Server administration default
8009	TCP		ajp13 – Apache JServ Protocol AJP Connector
8010	TCP		XMPP File transfers
8074	TCP		Gadu-Gadu
8075	TCP		Killing Floor
8080	TCP		HTTP alternate (http_alt) – commonly used for Web proxy and caching, or for running a Web server as a non-root user
8080	TCP		Apache Tomcat
8080		UDP	FilePhile Master/Relay
8081	TCP		HTTP alternate, VibeStreamer, e.g. McAfee ePolicy Orchestrator (ePO)
8086	TCP		HELM Web Host Automation Windows Control Panel
8086	TCP		Kaspersky AV Control Center
8087	TCP		Hosting Accelerator Control Panel
8087	TCP		Parallels Plesk Control Panel
8087		UDP	Kaspersky AV Control Center
8088	TCP		Asterisk (PBX) Web Configuration utility (GUI Addon)

8089	TCP		Splunk Daemon
8100	TCP		Console Gateway License Verification
8116		UDP	Check Point Cluster Control Protocol
8118	TCP		Privoxy–advertisement-filtering Web proxy
8123	TCP		Polipo Web proxy
8192-8194	TCP		Sophos Remote Management System
8200	TCP		GoToMyPC
8222	TCP		VMware Server Management User Interface (insecure Web interface). Also see port 8333
8243	TCP	UDP	HTTPS listener for Apache Synapse
8280	TCP	UDP	HTTP listener for Apache Synapse
8303		UDP	Teeworlds Server
8331	TCP		MultiBit,
8332	TCP		Bitcoin JSON-RPC server
8333	TCP		Bitcoin
8333	TCP		VMware Server Management User Interface (secure Web interface). Also see port 8222

8400	TCP	UDP	cvp, Commvault Unified Data Management
8442	TCP	UDP	CyBro A-bus, Cybrotech Ltd.
8443	TCP		SW Soft Plesk Control Panel, Apache Tomcat SSL, Promise WebPAM SSL, McAfee ePolicy Orchestrator (epO)
8484	TCP	UDP	MapleStory
8500	TCP	UDP	Macromedia/Adobe ColdFusion; Duke Nukem 3D
8601	TCP		Wavestore CCTV protocol
8602	TCP	UDP	Wavestore Notification protocol
8691	TCP		Ultra Fractal default server port for distributing calculations over network computers
8701		UDP	SoftPerfect Bandwidth Manager
8702		UDP	SoftPerfect Bandwidth Manager
8767		UDP	TeamSpeak – default
8768		UDP	TeamSpeak – alternate
8840	TCP		Opera Unite server
8880	TCP	UDP	cddbp-alt, CD DataBase (CDDB) protocol (CDDBP) alternate
8880	TCP		WebSphere Application Server SOAP connector default

8880	TCP		Win Media Streamer to Server SOAP connector default
8883	TCP	UDP	Secure MQ Telemetry Transport (MQTT over SSL)
8887	TCP		HyperVM HTTP
8888	TCP		HyperVM HTTPS
8888	TCP		Freenet HTTP
8888	TCP	UDP	NewsEDGE server
8888	TCP		GNUmp3d HTTP music streaming and Web interface
8888	TCP		LoLo Catcher HTTP Web interface
8888	TCP		D2GS Admin Console Telnet administration console for D2GS servers (Diablo 2)
8888	TCP		MAMP Server
8889	TCP		MAMP Server
9000	TCP		DBGp
9000	TCP		SqueezeCenter web server & streaming
9000		UDP	UDPCast
9001	TCP	UDP	ETL Service Manager
9001	TCP		Microsoft SharePoint authoring environment

9001	TCP		Tor network default
9001	TCP		DBGp Proxy
9009	TCP	UDP	Pichat Server–Peer to peer chat software
9010	TCP		TISERVICEMANAGEMENT Numara Track-It!
9020	TCP		WiT WiT Services
9025	TCP		WiT WiT Services
9030	TCP		Tor often used
9043	TCP		WebSphere Application Server Administration Console secure
9050	TCP		Tor
9051	TCP		Tor
9060	TCP		WebSphere Application Server Administration Console
9080		UDP	glrpc, Groove Collaboration software GLRPC
9080	TCP		glrpc, Groove Collaboration software GLRPC
9080	TCP		WebSphere Application Server HTTP Transport (port 1) default
9090	TCP		Openfire Administration Console
9090	TCP		SqueezeCenter control (CLI)

9091	TCP		Openfire Administration Console (SSL Secured)
9091	TCP		Transmission (BitTorrent client) Web Interface
9100	TCP		PDL Data Stream
9101	TCP	UDP	Bacula Director
9102	TCP	UDP	Bacula File Daemon
9103	TCP	UDP	Bacula Storage Daemon
9105	TCP	UDP	Xadmin Control Daemon
9106	TCP	UDP	Astergate Control Daemon
9107	TCP		Astergate-FAX Control Daemon
9110		UDP	SSMP Message protocol
9119	TCP	UDP	MXit Instant Messenger
9300	TCP		IBM Cognos 8 SOAP Business Intelligence and Performance Management
9303		UDP	D-Link Shareport Share storage and MFP printers
9306	TCP		Sphinx Native API
9312	TCP		Sphinx SphinxQL
9418	TCP	UDP	git, Git pack transfer service

9420	TCP		MooseFS distributed file system–master server to chunk servers
9421	TCP		MooseFS distributed file system–master server to clients
9422	TCP		MooseFS distributed file system–chunk servers to clients
9535	TCP	UDP	mngsuite, LANDesk Management Suite Remote Control
9536	TCP	UDP	laes-bf, IP Fabrics Surveillance buffering function
9600		UDP	Omron FINS, OMRON FINS PLC communication
9675	TCP	UDP	Spiceworks Desktop, IT Helpdesk Software
9676	TCP	UDP	Spiceworks Desktop, IT Helpdesk Software
9695		UDP	CCNx
9800	TCP	UDP	WebDAV Source
9800	TCP	UDP	WebCT e-learning portal
9875	TCP		Club Penguin Disney online game for kids
9987		UDP	TeamSpeak 3 server default (voice) port (for the conflicting service see the IANA list)

9996	TCP	UDP	The Palace "The Palace" Virtual Reality Chat software.-5
9998	TCP	UDP	The Palace "The Palace" Virtual Reality Chat software.-5
9999	TCP	UDP	Hydranode – edonkey2000 TELNET control
9999	TCP		Lantronix UDS-10/UDS100 RS-485 to Ethernet Converter TELNET control
10000	TCP		Webmin – Web-based Linux admin tool
10000	TCP		BackupExec
10001	TCP		Lantronix UDS-10/UDS100 RS-485 to Ethernet Converter default
10008	TCP	UDP	Octopus Multiplexer CROMP remoting protocol primary port
10010	TCP		Open Object Rexx (ooRexx) rxapi daemon
10050	TCP	UDP	Zabbix – Agent
10051	TCP	UDP	Zabbix – Trapper
10081	TCP		Zend Server administration
10110	TCP	UDP	NMEA 0183 Navigational Data
10113	TCP	UDP	NetIQ Endpoint
10114	TCP	UDP	NetIQ Qcheck

10115	TCP	UDP	NetIQ Endpoint
10116	TCP	UDP	NetIQ VoIP Assessor
10200–10204	TCP		FRISK Software International f-protd virus scanning daemon
11211	TCP	UDP	memcached
11371	TCP	UDP	OpenPGP HTTP key server
11576	TCP	UDP	IPStor Server management communication
12010	TCP		ElevateDB default database port
12012	TCP	UDP	Audition Online Dance Battle, Korea Server–Status/Version Check
12013	TCP	UDP	Audition Online Dance Battle, Korea Server
12222		UDP	Light Weight Access Point Protocol (LWAPP) LWAPP data (RFC 5412)
12223		UDP	Light Weight Access Point Protocol (LWAPP) LWAPP control (RFC 5412)
12345	TCP		NetBus–remote administration tool. Little Fighter 2 (TCP)
12975	TCP		LogMeIn Hamachi (VPN tunnel software; also port 32976)
13075	TCP		Default for BMC Software Control-M/Enterprise Manager Corba

13195-13196	TCP	UDP	Ontolux Ontolux 2D
13720	TCP	UDP	Symantec NetBackup–bprd (formerly VERITAS)
13721	TCP	UDP	Symantec NetBackup–bpdbm (formerly VERITAS)
13724	TCP	UDP	Symantec Network Utility–vnetd (formerly VERITAS)
13782	TCP	UDP	Symantec NetBackup–bpcd (formerly VERITAS)
13783	TCP	UDP	Symantec VOPIED protocol (formerly VERITAS)
13785	TCP	UDP	Symantec NetBackup Database–nbdb (formerly VERITAS)
13786	TCP	UDP	Symantec nomdb (formerly VERITAS)
14439	TCP		APRS UI-View Amateur Radio UI-WebServer
14567		UDP	Battlefield 1942 and mods
15000	TCP		psyBNC
15000	TCP		Wesnoth
15000	TCP	UDP	hydap, Hypack Hydrographic Software Packages Data Acquisition
15556	TCP	UDP	Jeex.EU Artesia (direct client-to-db.service)

15567		UDP	Battlefield Vietnam and mods
15345	TCP	UDP	XPilot Contact
16000	TCP		shroudBNC
16080	TCP		Mac OS X Server Web (HTTP) service with performance cache
16200	TCP		Oracle Universal Content Management Content Server
16250	TCP		Oracle Universal Content Management Inbound Refinery
16567		UDP	Battlefield 2 and mods
17500	TCP	UDP	Dropbox LanSync Protocol (db-lsp); used to synchronize file catalogs
18104	TCP		RAD PDF Service
18200	TCP	UDP	Audition Online Dance Battle, AsiaSoft Thailand Server – Status/Version Check
18201	TCP	UDP	Audition Online Dance Battle, AsiaSoft Thailand Server
18206	TCP	UDP	Audition Online Dance Battle, AsiaSoft Thailand Server – FAM Database
18300	TCP	UDP	Audition Online Dance Battle, AsiaSoft SEA Server – Status/Version Check

18301	TCP	UDP	Audition Online Dance Battle, AsiaSoft SEA Server
18306	TCP	UDP	Audition Online Dance Battle, AsiaSoft SEA Server – FAM Database
18333	TCP		Bitcoin testnet
18400	TCP	UDP	Audition Online Dance Battle, KAIZEN Brazil Server – Status/ Version Check
18401	TCP	UDP	Audition Online Dance Battle, KAIZEN Brazil Server
18505	TCP	UDP	Audition Online Dance Battle, Nexon Server – Status/Version Check
18506	TCP	UDP	Audition Online Dance Battle, Nexon Server
18605	TCP	UDP	X-BEAT – Status/Version Check
18606	TCP	UDP	X-BEAT
19000	TCP	UDP	Audition Online Dance Battle, G10/ alaplaya Server – Status/Version Check
19001	TCP	UDP	Audition Online Dance Battle, G10/ alaplaya Server
19226	TCP		Panda Software AdminSecure Communication Agent

19283	TCP	UDP	K2 - KeyAuditor & KeyServer, Sassafras Software Inc. Software Asset Management tools
19294	TCP		Google Talk Voice and Video connections
19295		UDP	Google Talk Voice and Video connections
19302		UDP	Google Talk Voice and Video connections
19315	TCP	UDP	KeyShadow for K2 – KeyAuditor & KeyServer, Sassafras Software Inc. Software Asset Management tools
19999	TCP	UDP	Distributed Network Protocol (DNP) – Secure, a secure version of the protocol used in SCADA systems between communicating RTUs and IEDs
20000	TCP	UDP	DNP (Distributed Network Protocol), a protocol used in SCADA systems between communicating RTUs and IEDs
20000	TCP	UDP	Usermin, Web-based user tool
20560	TCP	UDP	Killing Floor
20720	TCP		Symantec i3 Web GUI server
21001	TCP		AMLFilter, AMLFilter Inc. amlf-admin default port

21011	TCP		AMLFilter, AMLFilter Inc. amlf-engine-01 default http port
21012	TCP		AMLFilter, AMLFilter Inc. amlf-engine-01 default https port
21021	TCP		AMLFilter, AMLFilter Inc. amlf-engine-02 default http port
21022	TCP		AMLFilter, AMLFilter Inc. amlf-engine-02 default https port
22136	TCP		FLIR Systems Camera Resource Protocol
22222	TCP		Davis Instruments, WeatherLink IP
22347	TCP	UDP	WibuKey, WIBU-SYSTEMS AG Software protection system
22349	TCP		Wolfson Microelectronics WISCEBridge Debug Protocol
22350	TCP	UDP	CodeMeter, WIBU-SYSTEMS AG Software protection system
23073	TCP	UDP	Soldat Dedicated Server
23399	TCP	UDP	Skype Default Protocol
23513	TCP	UDP	Duke Nukem 3D
24444	TCP	UDP	NetBeans integrated development environment
24465	TCP	UDP	Tonido Directory Server for Tonido – a Personal Web App and P2P platform

24554	TCP	UDP	BINKP, Fidonet mail transfers over TCP/IP
24800	TCP	UDP	Synergy: keyboard/mouse sharing software
24842	TCP	UDP	StepMania: Online: Dance Dance Revolution Simulator
25000	TCP		Teamware Office standard client connection
25003	TCP		Teamware Office client notifier
25005	TCP		Teamware Office message transfer
25007	TCP		Teamware Office MIME Connector
25010	TCP		Teamware Office Agent server
25565	TCP		Minecraft Dedicated Server
25826		UDP	collectd default port
25888		UDP	Xfire (Firewall Report, UDP_IN)
25999	TCP		Xfire
26000		UDP	id Software's Quake server
26000	TCP		id Software's Quake server
26000	TCP		CCP's EVE Online Online gaming MMORPG
26900	TCP		CCP's EVE Online Online gaming MMORPG

26901	TCP		CCP's EVE Online Online gaming MMORPG
27000		UDP	(through 27006) id Software's QuakeWorld master server
27000-27009	TCP		FlexNet Publisher's License server (range of default ports)
27010	TCP	UDP	Half-Life
27015	TCP	UDP	Half-Life
27016	TCP	UDP	Magicka server port
27017	TCP		mongoDB server port
27374	TCP	UDP	Sub7 default
27500-27900		UDP	id Software's QuakeWorld
27888		UDP	Kaillera server
27900-27901			Nintendo Wi-Fi Connection
27901-27910		UDP	id Software's Quake II master server
27950		UDP	OpenArena outgoing
27960-27969		UDP	Activision's Enemy Territory and id Software's Quake III Arena, Quake III and Quake Live and some io-quake3 derived games (OpenArena incoming)

28000	TCP		NX License Manager
28001	TCP	UDP	Starsiege: Tribes Common/default Tribes v.1 Server
28785		UDP	Cube 2 Sauerbraten
28786		UDP	Cube 2 Sauerbraten Port 2
28852	TCP	UDP	Killing Floor
28960		UDP	Call of Duty; Call of Duty: United Offensive; Call of Duty 2; Call of Duty 4: Modern Warfare; Call of Duty: World at War (PC Version)
29000	TCP	UDP	Perfect World International Used by the Perfect World International Client
30000	TCP	UDP	Pokémon Netbattle
30301	TCP		BitTorrent
30564	TCP		Multiplicity: keyboard/mouse/clipboard sharing software
30718		UDP	Lantronix Discovery for Lantronix serial-to-ethernet devices
30777	TCP		ZangZing agent
31337	TCP		Back Orifice – remote administration tool (often Trojan horse)
31415	TCP	UDP	ThoughtSignal – Server Communication Service

31456	TCP		TetriNET IRC gateway on some servers
31457	TCP		TetriNET
31458	TCP		TetriNET Used for game spectators
31620	TCP	UDP	LM-MON (Standard Floating License Manager LM-MON)
32123	TCP		x3Lobby
32245	TCP		MMTSG – mutilated over MMT (encrypted transmission)
32769	TCP		FileNet RPC
32976	TCP		LogMeIn Hamachi (VPN tunnel software; also port 12975)
33434	TCP	UDP	traceroute
33982	TCP	UDP	Dezta software
34567	TCP		EDI service
36963		UDP	USGN online games, most notably Counter Strike 2D multiplayer (2D clone of popular CounterStrike computer game)
40000	TCP	UDP	SafetyNET p Real-time Industrial Ethernet protocol
43594–43595	TCP		Jagex, RuneScape, FunOrb

47001	TCP		WinRM - Windows Remote Management Service
47808	TCP	UDP	BACnet Building Automation and Control Networks

Appendix III: Units of Measure for Digital Information

The smallest unit of digital information is binary digit or *bit*. A bit has two possible values *0* and *1*. The shorthand for bit is lowercase "b".

Eight bits form one *byte*. The shorthand for byte is uppercase "B".

$$1 \text{ byte} = 8 \text{ bits} \qquad 1 \text{ B} = 8 \text{ b}$$
$$16 \text{ bits} = 2 \text{ bytes} \qquad 16 \text{ b} = 2 \text{ B}$$

Binary numbers are written with ones and zeroes. Hexadecimal system is popular when dealing with computers, as a group of four binary digits (bits) is compactly represented by one hexadecimal digit.

Decimal	Binary	Hexadecimal
0	0000	0h
1	0001	1h
2	0010	2h
3	0011	3h
4	0100	4h
5	0101	5h
6	0110	6h
7	0111	7h
8	1000	8h
9	1001	9h
10	1010	Ah
11	1011	Bh
12	1100	Ch
13	1101	Dh
14	1110	Eh
15	1111	Fh

To convert a binary number to hexadecimal, simply separate bits into groups of four, starting with the least significant (add up to three leading zeroes to the leftmost group as needed). And then for each of the four bit groups write one corresponding hexadecimal digit from the table above.

For example:

111111100101100 = 0111 1111 0010 1100 = 7 F 2 C = 7F2Ch

To convert a hexadecimal number into binary form, the procedure is reverse. For each hexadecimal digit, write four binary ones from the table, and then delete any leading zeroes, if desired.

7F2Ch = 7 F 2 C = 0111 1111 0010 1100 = 111111100101100

The trailing "h" at the end of hexadecimal numbers simply denotes the numbers as hexadecimal. This is one of the popular notations. The "h" is needed so that not to confuse hexadecimal numbers with decimal (or other base) numbers as hexadecimal numbers do not always contain letters. For example:

$$100100110 = 0001\ 0010\ 0110 = 126h = 294$$

Another popular way, used when writing numbers of different bases, is specifying the base in subscript, often enclosing the number in parenthesis for more clarity:

$$(100100110)_2 = (126)_{16} = (294)_{10}$$

There are, of course, other bases besides binary, hexadecimal, and decimal. But these three are the most popular in information technology.

Now that we looked at numbers, let us examine what happens with number multiplication prefixes.

Prefixes in the scientific world confirm to the International System of Units (SI) and are powers of ten. As such we have kilometer, which is one thousand meters, we have milligram – one-thousandth of a gram; and many other multiples.

Since computers internally work with binary numbers – numbers with base of two – computer specialists have traditionally operated with powers of two rather than powers of ten. As such, one kilobyte is equal 1024 bytes, when using power of two multipliers; versus 1000 bytes with power of ten multipliers. Two to the power of ten is 1024, where ten to the power of three is 1000.

As you can imagine, the usage of the same prefixes to indicate sometimes the powers of ten while other times – the powers of two, created a lot of confusion. The most notable effort to clearly differentiate between binary and decimal prefixes had been spearheaded by the International Electrotechnical Commission (IEC).

Other standards bodies, including the United States National Institute of Standards and Technology (NIST), the Institute of Electrical and Electronics Engineers (IEEE) Standards Association, and the European Committee for Electrotechnical Standardization (CENELEC), also adapted the IEC recommendation.

The general idea of the IEC system is to keep the traditional kilo, mega, giga, tera, peta, exa, zetta, and yotta as decimal prefixes only. The new prefixes: kibi, mebi, gibi, tebi, pebi, exbi, zebi, and yobi are created for binary multipliers. As such:

    1 kilobyte = 1000 bytes
    1 kibibyte = 1024 bytes

Adaptation of the IEC standard has been slow. We have yet to see the new binary prefixes in wide use.

Manufacturers who have already used the traditional prefixes to indicate powers of ten – notably hard drive and other non-volatile storage (except for diskettes and early compact disks) device manufacturers – became compliant with the new standard by default. Data transmission and clock rates are always specified with decimal prefixes. At the same time, memory chips manufacturers, that used the traditional prefixes to indicate powers of two, continued with the legacy practice.

User interfaces of many operating systems, including Windows 2008 R2, also continue to use the legacy prefixes when displaying file sizes. For example, place a file that is exactly 1,048,576 bytes into a folder and instruct Windows Explorer to show details (click and release the "Alt" key, then choose "View – Details" from the main menu), you will see the file size reported as "1,024 KB."

Furthermore, right click on the file, and chose "Properties" from the pop-up menu. In the "General" tab of the file properties dialog you will see the file size reported as

$$1.00 \text{ MB } (1,048,576 \text{ bytes})$$

In the legacy system:

$$1,048,576 \text{ B} = 1,024 \text{ kB} = 1 \text{ MB}$$

In the IEC system:

$$1,048,576 \text{ B} = 1,024 \text{ KiB} = 1 \text{ MiB}$$
$$1,000,000 \text{ B} = 1,000 \text{ kB} = 1 \text{ MB}$$

The table that follows will help you to find the exact values for multiplier prefixes in both legacy and IEC systems.

Multiplier Prefixes Table

Exponents		Numbers			Scale		Prefixes	
$(2^{10})^m$	$(10^3)^n$	Decimal	Hexadecimal	Binary	Short	Long	Legacy	IEC
0	0	1	1h	1	One	One		
	1	1000	3E8h	1111101000	Thousand	Thousand	kilo (k)	kilo (k)
1		1024	400h	10000000000				kibi (Ki)
	2	1000000	F4240h	11110100001001000000	Million	Million	mega (M)	mega (M)
2		1048576	100000h	100000000000000000000				mebi (Mi)
	3	1000000000	3B9ACA00h	A 30-digit binary number	Billion*	Milliard	giga (G)	giga (G)
3		1073741824	40000000h	One and 30 zeros				gibi (Gi)
	4	1000000000000	E8D4A51000h	A 40-digit binary number	Trillion	Billion	tera (T)	tera (T)
4		1095511627776	10000000000h	One and 40 zeros				tebi (Ti)
	5	1000000000000000	38D7EA4C68000h	A 50-digit binary number	Quadrillion	Billiard	peta (P)	peta (P)
5		1125899906842624	4000000000000h	One and 50 zeros				pebi (Pi)
	6	1000000000000000000	DE0B6B3A7640000h	A 60-digit binary number	Quintillion	Trillion	exa (E)	exa (E)
6		1152921504606846976	1000000000000000h	One and 60 zeros				exbi (Ei)
	7	1000000000000000000000	3635C9ADC5DEA00000h	A 70-digit binary number	Sextillion	Trilliard	zetta (Z)	zetta (Z)
7		1180591620717411303424	400000000000000000h	One and 70 zeros				zebi (Zi)
	8	1000000000000000000000000	D3C21BCECCEDA1000000h	An 80-digit binary number	Septillion	Quadrillion	yotta (Y)	yotta (Y)
8		1208925819614629174706176	100000000000000000000h	One and 80 zeros				yobi (Yi)

* The short scale is in use in the United Sates and most English speaking nations. A few countries (including Albania, Bulgaria, Egypt, Indonesia, Iran, Israel, Saudi Arabia, Turkey, Russia and other parts of the former Soviet Union) utilize the short scale but use the word *Milliard (or similar)* instead of, or in addition to, the word *Billion*. Further country-specific variations may exist.